TO THE WRITER WHO SURVIVES ALL THIS;
AND TO THE FINAL CRITIC,
THE UNSUNG READER

PUSHCART'S
COMPLETE

ROTTEN
REVIEWS
&
REJECTIONS

EDITED BY
BILL HENDERSON & ANDRÉ BERNARD

DESIGNED AND ILLUSTRATED BY
MARY KORNBLUM

INTRODUCTIONS BY
ANTHONY BRANDT & BILL HENDERSON

PUSHCART PRESS
WAINSCOTT, NEW YORK 11975

ISBN 0-888889-04-7

Distributed by W.W. Norton & Co.
500 Fifth Avenue
New York, NY 10110

With thanks to Jim Charlton and Jon Richards — editors.

For Walt Whitman,
who may have written
some of his best reviews
himself.

ROTTEN REVIEWS

BILL HENDERSON
EDITOR

Rotten Reviews is for all writers who spent years, if not a lifetime, writing a book and then had it dismissed by a rotten review.

Rotten reviews have happened to some of the best books and authors, and here are a few of them, with their detractors.

In determining the best books and authors I let history have the final say. Each of these books has lasted for at least ten years and some have been respected for centuries. Under the heading of Review, I have included not only periodical reviews but critical essays, diary entries, letters and reported conversation.

While researching this modest survey, I was impressed by the balance, intelligence and fairness of most reviewers. The truly malicious review was a rarity.

Often reviewers went into spasms of appreciation for books of slight value: "Martin Tupper (1810-1889) has won for himself the vacant throne waiting for him amidst the immortals, and has been adopted by the suffrage of mankind and the final decrees of publishers into the same rank with Wordsworth, Tennyson and Browning." The Spectator (1866)

Even bad reviews were appreciated. When the Concord Massachusetts public library banned Huckleberry Finn, Mark Twain exulted: "That will sell 25,000 books for sure!"

Rotten Reviews is not a scholarly study. When available I have quoted from the original documents, but often review digests, critical text editions and biographies were the source of the bad blurb. In each case, the opinion cited appeared about the time of the book's publication, unless otherwise noted. I have concentrated on English, European and American literature, which leaves out a whole world of ill-will from other countries.

BILL HENDERSON

A couple of years ago I was asked to review a minor work by a well-known writer, and, after some hesitation, accepted the assignment. I hesitated because, although I did not know the writer, we shared a friend, a man I shall call Don; and Don was passionately committed to this woman's work and thought her without parallel among contemporary novelists. Suppose I didn't like the book? How would Don react? Don and I weren't close but I did respect him. I thought he was a better writer, in fact, than his esteemed lady friend, and I didn't particularly want to alienate him for the sake of such a slender, inconsequential thing as a book review.

Nevertheless I took the assignment, the book came in the mail, it turned out to be dreadful, insensitive and superficial in the extreme, and I swallowed hard and gave it a rotten review. A few weeks later, shortly after the review had appeared, I walked into the local bar where both Don and I hang out; there was Don, sitting at a table with some friends. I went over to say hello and he gave me a long, hard stare. "Ah," he said finally, "it's the Reviewer." He hasn't spoken to me since.

I got off easy, of course. One friend lost is nothing. Other Reviewers lose whole continents of friends. Still others get anonymous threats in the mail. There have been cases of actual physical assault; one irate author threw a Reviewer I know down a flight of stairs. All are regularly subject to long letters impugning their intelligence, their integrity, their humanity, which letters appear in the very publications that employ them. And for what? Reviewing will never make one rich. The enemies one makes writing reviews will almost inevitably seek revenge if one should be so foolish as to publish one's own books. And one may very well wind up someday immortalized in sly little anthologies like this, egg permanently smeared all over one's face, because one thought a minor work by a well-known writer was insensitive and superficial in the extreme and it has turned out to be—who could have guessed it?—a classic.

It is enough to give one pause. It is enough, indeed, to incline one to abandon reviewing altogether. Who would want to have called *Wuthering Heights*, not too long after it had appeared, "a crude and morbid story," or to have said about Dickens and one of his greatest novels, *Our Mutual Friend*, that "We are convinced that it is one of the chief conditions of his genius not to see beneath the surface of things. . . . We are aware that this definition confines him to an inferior rank."? That it was Henry James who made these remarks only reinforces the point. If great writers can be wrong about other great writers, how do mere Reviewers summon the nerve to pass judgments? One of the pleasures of this wicked collection is watching the great being terribly wrong about the great. Emile Zola is here terribly wrong about Baudelaire, Gertrude Stein about Ezra Pound, Emerson about Jane Austen, Edmund Wilson about W. H. Auden, George Bernard Shaw about Shakespeare, and just about everybody about Walt Whitman. A pleasure, but an intimidating one. Why reveal one's blindnesses in this way? The risks of reviewing are clearly considerable, the rewards minimal. Why do it?

One does it, I suppose, for a number of submerged reasons that don't look particularly attractive in the light. One of them, obviously, is that it gives one a sense of power to pass judgment on the works of others and become an arbiter of taste. Another is the satisfaction of being clever at someone else's expense. "Writers," notes Saul Bellow, "seldom wish other writers well." Indeed it is a long tradition to take one's fellows amusingly apart in public. Aristophanes did it to his fellow dramatists, Alexander Pope to his fellow poets. In late Medieval times the tradition was formalized in the verse fliting, a war of words, poet against poet, may the most outrageous insults win. The impulse remains the same; now we are merely more indirect. We write reviews.

Not that all reviews are rotten. Far from it. In fact, when the reviewing of books first became common practice in the United States, in the 1840s, it was quite rare to find a rotten review of any book, however egregious a production it may have been. We must not assume, however, that this was some golden age of concord between authors and Reviewers. The concord was entirely between publishers and newspapers, the former paying the latter, by one quiet means or another, for favorable reviews.

The system fell apart in 1855 when an anonymous Reviewer for the *Boston Daily Evening Traveller* called Longfellow's *Hiawatha* "childish nonsense" and regretted that our "pet national poet" could find no better subject for his muse "than the silly legends of the savage aborigines." This so outraged Longfellow's publisher, James T. Fields, that he wrote the *Traveller* and indignantly removed all his advertising from the paper. The *Traveller* promptly printed Fields' letter under the title, "Attempt to Coerce the Press." A few weeks later a publisher's newsletter attacked the *Traveller* and defended Fields, admitting in the process that if publishers "seek to bribe the press . . . it is from necessity, not choice." For the press, according to the publishers, demanded to be bribed. " 'Give us advertisements and we will give good notices' is a proposition made every day to publishers," said the publishers. With the fat now in the fire there was no way to avoid a general conflagration. Several eminent Reviewers were discovered to be salaried employees of the publishers whose books they were reviewing. Some publishers had been helpfully sending to newspapers along with their books unsigned reviews that they themselves had written, with the helpful hint that the papers were free to use these reviews however they wished. It was all terribly scandalous and it had to stop.

Some publishers, I'm sure, still think there should be no rotten reviews. Some writers think so, too. Kurt Vonnegut is known to believe that no one should review fiction badly. Anthony Burgess said recently in *TLS* (replying at length to a rotten review of one of his own books) that "In my capacity as critic I never stab anybody, for I know how life-denying it is to be stabbed. Writing a book is damned difficult work, and you ought to praise any book if you can." Burgess was sufficiently worldly to add, however, that "praise is a bland commodity and readers don't like to read it." Indeed. No one would publish an anthology of wonderful reviews of worthless authors, plentiful as they are; no, we get only devilish entertainments like this. Which is another reason why Reviewers do it. They have their public, too; they know what that public demands. And the public must be served.

Not that Reviewers earn much respect for their work, even from the public they try so hard to satisfy. Even, at times, from themselves. "We are generally a poor lot," wrote the sometime Reviewer Leslie Stephen to his friend Thomas Hardy, "horribly afraid of not being in the fashion, and disposed to give ourselves airs on very small grounds." Evidence exists that Reviewers have only a small impact on the sale of books; a study in West Germany some years ago indicated that word-of-mouth sold books at twice the rate of reviews. Certainly bad reviews are no restraint on the sale of James Michener's books, as they were not on those of Jacqueline Susann's, or Frances Parkinson Keyes', or Susan Warner's. (Who were these people? you ask. *Sic transit gloria mundi.*) This does not prevent authors from hating Reviewers and taking their revenge as only they know how. It is well known what Pope did to Colley Cibber in the *Dunciad.* Byron wrote a whole poem satirizing Scotch Reviewers, and it made him famous. The eminent writer I reviewed took her revenge on me, writing a scathing letter to the publication my Review appeared in indicating that I had no sense of humor. Naturally the publication printed it.

All of this has a serious side, as the rage of my particular Reviewee attests. Rotten reviews hurt, for one thing. And if they don't, perhaps, affect sales, they do affect literary reputations, which, as most authors will agree, are more important than sales in the end. This anthology would seem to demonstrate that ultimately it doesn't matter; the good will drive out the bad, Melville endures while the Reviewers who made his life a torment are long forgotten. Perhaps. But how many great talents have been rendered mute and inglorious because, early on, Reviewers accused them of "sophistry," or of attacking "the most sacred associations of life," or of being "dangerous"? These were some of the milder epithets levelled at Melville. The man stopped writing, remember, for nearly forty years.

But now he has his revenge, and we his readers can take our vicarious pleasure in it. We have all, writers and non-writers alike, received bad notices of one sort or another. Our bosses criticize our work, our wives or our husbands walk out on us, our children wonder out loud how on earth we ever made it to adulthood. A friend of mine has on his refrigerator a sign that reads, "Avenge yourself. Live long enough to become a problem to your children." Write well enough that someday your Reviewers will look like fools. Especially the famous ones, great writers themselves, who turned out to be terribly wrong about you.

That is the chief pleasure of this little book, the vision of history setting things right, the judgment of the ages settling old scores. But it is not necessarily a simple pleasure. As an occasional Reviewer it behooves me to point out that some of these rotten reviews have a twist to them. When Virginia Woolf declares James Joyce's *Ulysses* a "misfire," we smile, but it is a crooked smile, for how many of us have actually been able to read *Ulysses* all the way through? How many of us have found this or that classic boring and unpalatable? George Eliot observed in her notebook that "a man who dares to say that he finds an eminent classic feeble here, extravagant there, and in general overrated, may chance to give an opinion which has some genuine discrimination in it concerning a new work or a living thinker—an opinion such as can hardly ever be got from the reputed judge who is a correct echo of the most approved phrases concerning those who have been already canonized."

It is the new work or the living thinker Reviewers primarily are called upon to judge, and it takes a certain courage on their part to be willing to be wrong. They are a poor lot indeed, ill-paid, despised all around, and often wrong, but they have their pride. Smile, then, but let it be a crooked smile; and ask yourself as you look at these rotten reviews whether you would have had the courage or the insight in 1855, say, to recognize the greatness of the author of *Leaves of Grass* when the rest of the literary world, almost to a man, was calling him a clown.

ANTHONY BRANDT

I

ROTTEN REVIEWS

...SINCE 411 BC

WINESBURG, OHIO
SHERWOOD ANDERSON
1918

We sympathize with Mr. Anderson and with what he is trying to do. He tries to find honest mid-American gods. Yet either he never does quite find them or he can never precisely set forth what he has found. It seems probable that he caricatures even Winesburg, Ohio.

The Nation

ON
MATTHEW ARNOLD

Arnold is a dandy Isaiah, a poet without passion, whose verse, written in surplice, is for freshmen and for gentle maidens who will be wooed to the arms of these future rectors.

George Meredith, *Fortnightly Review*   1909

ON
W.H. AUDEN

Mr. Auden himself has presented the curious case of a poet who writes an original poetic language in the most robust English tradition but who seems to have been arrested in the mentality of an adolescent schoolboy.

Edmund Wilson, *The Shores of Light*   1952

PRIDE
AND PREJUDICE
JANE AUSTEN
1813

Why do you like Miss Austen so very much? I am puzzled on that point . . . I should hardly like to live with her ladies and gentlemen, in their elegant but confined houses . . . Miss Austen is only shrewd and observant.

Charlotte Brontë, letter to G.H. Lewes   1848

ON
JANE AUSTEN

Mama says that she was then the prettiest, silliest, most affected, husband-hunting butterfly she ever remembers.

Mary Russell Mitford, letter to Sir William Etford   1815

I am at a loss to understand why people hold Miss Austen's novels at so high a rate, which seem to me vulgar in tone, sterile in artistic invention, imprisoned in the wretched conventions of English society, without genius, wit, or knowledge of the world. Never was life so pinched and narrow. The one problem in the mind of the writer . . . is marriageableness . . . Suicide is more respectable.

Ralph Waldo Emerson, *Journal*   1861

ON

FRANCIS BACON

His faults were—we write it with pain—coldness of heart, and meanness of spirit. He seems to have been incapable of feeling strong affection, of facing great dangers, of making great sacrifices. His desires were set on things below, titles, patronage, the mace, the seals, the coronet, large houses, fair gardens, rich manors, many services of pate . . ."

T.B. Macaulay, *Essays* 1842

ON

HONORÉ DE BALZAC

Little imagination is shown in invention, in the creating of character and plot, or in the delineation of passion . . . M. de Balzac's place in French literature will be neither considerable nor high.

Eugene Poitou, *Revue des Deux Mondes* 1856

THE END OF THE ROAD
JOHN BARTH
1958

The same road that has been travelled with Kerouac and to an extent Herbert Gold, this is for those schooled in the waste matter of the body and the mind; for others, a real recoil.

Kirkus Reviews

LES FLEURS DU MAL
CHARLES BAUDELAIRE
1857

In a hundred years the histories of French literature will only mention (this work) as a curio.

Emile Zola, in *Emile Zola*   1953

MOLLOY; MALONE DIES;
THE UNNAMEABLE
SAMUEL BECKETT
1959
(three novels in one volume)

In attempting to depict the boredom of human existence, he has run the very grave risk of thoroughly boring his reader.

San Francisco Chronicle

The suggestion that something larger is being said about the human predicament . . . won't hold water, any more than Beckett's incontinent heroes can.

The Spectator

ON
MAX BEERBOHM

He is a shallow, affected, self-conscious fribble—so there.

Vita Sackville-West, letter to Harold Nicolson   1959

DANGLING MAN
SAUL BELLOW
1944

As the publishers say, it is a sympathetic and understanding study of a young man struggling with his soul. It might be even more sympathetic if Author Bellow (who is not in the Army) ever seemed to suspect that, as an object of pity, his hero is a pharisaical stinker.

Time

WUTHERING HEIGHTS
EMILY BRONTË
1847

Here all the faults of *Jane Eyre* (by Charlotte Brontë) are magnified a thousand fold, and the only consolation which we have in reflecting upon it is that it will never be generally read.

James Lorimer, *North British Review*

. . . wild, confused, disjointed and improbable . . . the people who make up the drama, which is tragic enough in its consequences, are savages ruder than those who lived before the days of Homer.

The Examiner

THE GOOD EARTH
PEARL BUCK
1931

Since Mrs. Buck does not understand the meaning of the Confucian separation of man's kingdom from that of woman, she is like someone trying to write a story of the European Middle Ages without understanding the rudiments of chivalric standards and the institution of Christianity.

New Republic

ON
LORD BYRON

His versification is so destitute of sustained harmony, many of his thoughts are so strained, his sentiments so unamiable, his misanthropy so gloomy, his libertinism so shameless, his merriment such a grinning of a ghastly smile, that I have always believed his verses would soon rank with forgotten things.

John Quincy Adams, *Memoirs*   1830

THE FALL
ALBERT CAMUS
1957

The style is unattractive if apt, being the oblique and stilted flow of a man working his way round to asking for a loan. There is a good deal of jaded Bohemian rot about the bourgeoisie being worse than professional criminals (are we not all guilty, etc.) and outbursts of cynical anguish about platitudes, e.g. 'don't believe your friends when they ask you to be sincere with them.' One might define stupidity as the state of needing to be told this.

Anthony Quinton, *New Statesman*

ALICE IN WONDERLAND
LEWIS CARROLL
1865

We fancy that any real child might be more puzzled than enchanted by this stiff, overwrought story.

Children's Books

JOURNEY TO THE END OF THE NIGHT
LOUIS FERDINAND CÉLINE
1934

Most readers will find *Journey to The End of The Night* a revolting book; its vision of human life will seem to them a hideous nightmare. It does not carry within itself adequate compensation for the bruising and battering of spirit with which one reads it: there is no purgative effect from all these disgusts. If this is life, then it is better not to live.

J.D. Adams, *New York Times Book Review*

DEATH ON THE INSTALLMENT PLAN
LOUIS FERDINAND CÉLINE
1938

Its effect is to make sympathy, then to put sympathy to sleep, then to exacerbate the nerves of the reader, until, having decided he has as much as he wants to stomach, he throws the book away.

Times Literary Supplement

ON
CHAUCER

Chaucer, not withstanding the praises bestowed on him, I think obscene and contemptible: he owes his celebrity merely to his antiquity, which he does not deserve so well as Piers Plowman or Thomas Erceldoune.

Lord Byron, *The Works of Lord Byron*   1835

UNCLE VANYA
ANTON CHEKHOV
PERFORMED IN NEW YORK, 1949

If you were to ask me what *Uncle Vanya* is about, I would say about as much as I can take.

Robert Garland, *Journal American*

THE AWAKENING
KATE CHOPIN
1899

That this book is strong and that Miss Chopin has a keen knowledge of certain phases of the feminine will not be denied. But it was not necessary for a writer of so great refinement and poetic grace to enter the overworked field of sex fiction.

Chicago Times-Herald

ON
SAMUEL TAYLOR COLERIDGE

We cannot name one considerable poem of his that is likely to remain upon the thresh-floor of fame ... We fear we shall seem to our children to have been pigmies, indeed, in intellect, since a man as Coleridge would appear great to us!

London Weekly Review   1828

YOUTH *and* HEART OF DARKNESS
JOSEPH CONRAD
1902

It would be useless to pretend that they can be very widely read.

Manchester Guardian

Mark Twain keeps score.

THE DEERSLAYER
JAMES FENIMORE COOPER
1841

In one place in Deerslayer, and in the restricted space of two-thirds of a page, Cooper has scored 114 offences against literary art out of a possible 115. It breaks the record.

Mark Twain, *How to Tell A Story and Other Essays* 1897

THE BRIDGE
HART CRANE
1932

A form of hysteria . . . One thing he has demonstrated, the impossibility of getting anywhere with the Whitmanian inspiration. No writer of comparable ability has struggled with it before and it seems highly unlikely that any writer of comparable genius will struggle with it again.

Yvor Winters, *Poetry*

MAGGIE: A GIRL OF THE STREETS
STEPHEN CRANE
1893

. . . we should classify Mr. Crane as a rather promising writer of the animalistic school. His types are mainly human beings of the order which makes us regret the

31

power of literature to portray them. Not merely are they low, but there is little that is interesting in them.

The Nation

BLEAK HOUSE
CHARLES DICKENS
1853

More than any of its predecessors chargeable with not simply faults, but absolute want of construction . . . meagre and melodramatic.

George Brimley, *The Spectator*

A TALE OF TWO CITIES
CHARLES DICKENS
1859

Last winter I forced myself through his *Tale of Two Cities*. It was a sheer dead pull from start to finish. It all seemed so insincere, such a transparent make-believe, a mere piece of acting.

John Burroughs, *Century Magazine* 1897

ON
CHARLES DICKENS

We do not believe in the permanence of his reputation . . . Fifty years hence, most of his allusions will be harder to understand than the allusions in *The Dunciad*, and our children will wonder what their ancestors could have meant by putting Mr. Dickens at the head of the novelists of his day.

Saturday Review 1858

ON
EMILY DICKINSON

An eccentric, dreamy, half-educated recluse in an out-of-the-way New England village—or anywhere else—cannot with impunity set at defiance the laws of gravitation and grammar . . . Oblivion lingers in the immediate neighborhood.

Thomas Bailey Aldrich, *Atlantic Monthly* 1892

ON
JOHN DONNE

Of his earlier poems, many are very licentious; the later are chiefly devout. Few are good for much.

Henry Hallam, *Introduction to the Literature of Europe* 1837

THE 42nd PARALLEL
JOHN DOS PASSOS
1930

. . . he is like a man who is trying to run in a dozen directions at once, succeeding thereby merely in standing still and making a noise. Sometimes it is amusing noise and alive; often monotonous.

V.S. Pritchett, *The Spectator*

THE BIG MONEY
JOHN DOS PASSOS
1936

I found the novel tiresome because people never seemed to matter in the least; they would have gone down under any system, so why blame capitalism for their complete and appalling lack of character? Mr. Dos Passos' America seems to me a figment of his own imagination, and I doubt the value of his reportage of our period.

Herschel Bricknell, *Review of Reviews*

AN AMERICAN TRAGEDY
THEODORE DREISER
1925

The commonplaceness of the story is not alleviated in the slightest degree by any glimmer of imaginative insight on the part of the novelist. A skillful writer would be able to arouse an emotional reaction in the reader but at no moment does he leave him otherwise than cold and unresponsive. One feature of the novel stands out above all others—the figure of Clyde Griffiths. If the novel were great, he would be a great character. As it is, he is certainly one of the most despicable creations of humanity that ever emerged from a novelist's brain. Last of all, it may be said without fear of contradiction that Mr. Dreiser is a fearsome manipulator of the English language. His style, if style it may be called, is offensively colloquial, commonplace and vulgar.

Boston Evening Transcript

MIDDLEMARCH
GEORGE ELIOT
1871-72

Middlemarch is a treasure-house of details, but it is an indifferent whole.

Henry James, *Galaxy*

THE WASTE LAND
T.S. ELIOT
1922

Mr. Eliot has shown that he can at moments write real blank verse; but that is all. For the rest he has quoted a great deal, he has parodied and imitated. But the parodies are cheap and the imitations inferior.

New Statesman

. . . it is the finest horses which have the most tender mouths and some unsympathetic tug has sent Mr. Eliot's

Mr. Eliot practices equitation.

gift awry. When he recovers control we shall expect his poetry to have gained in variety and strength from this ambitious experiment.

Times Literary Supplement

THE COCKTAIL PARTY
T.S. ELIOT
PERFORMED AT EDINBURGH FESTIVAL, 1949

The week after—as well as the morning after—I take it to be nothing but a finely acted piece of flapdoodle.

Alan Dent, *News Chronicle*

ON
RALPH WALDO EMERSON

A hoary-headed and toothless baboon.

Thomas Carlyle, *Collected Works* 1871

Belongs to a class of gentlemen with whom we have no patience whatever—the mystics for mysticism's sake . . . The best answer to his twaddle is *cui bono?*—a very little Latin phrase very generally mistranslated and misunder-stood—*cui bono?* to whom is it a benefit? If not to Mr. Emerson individually, then surely to no man.

Edgar Allan Poe, in a chapter of autobiography 1842

Poe answers twaddle.

ON
EURIPIDES

A cliché anthologist ... and maker of ragamuffin manikins.

Aristophanes, *The Thesmophoriazusae*   411 B.C.

**LET US NOW PRAISE
FAMOUS MEN**
WALKER EVANS   JAMES AGEE
1941

There are many objectionable passages and references. I am sorry not to be able to recommend this book for the subject is an important one.

L.R. Etzkorn, *Library Journal*

**THE YOUNG MANHOOD OF
STUDS LONIGAN**
JAMES T. FARRELL
1934

Unfortunately the author's interest in attempting to shock his readers appears to be greater than his interest in an accurate characterization of the young men around whom this story is developed.

American Journal of Sociology

A case history, true for this boy Studs Lonigan, but not completely valid as the recreation of a social stratum which it also would seem to aim at being.

New York Times Book Review

AS I LAY DYING
WILLIAM FAULKNER
1930

. . . the critic can hardly be blamed if some categorical imperative which persists in the human condition (even at this late date) compels him to put his book in a high place in an inferior category.

New York Times Book Review

LIGHT IN AUGUST
WILLIAM FAULKNER
1932

Despite Mr. Faulkner's great gifts and deep sensitivity, what he is actually offering us is a flight from reality. It's horrors and obscenities in no way contradict this, for many persons, tired of ordinary life, have been known to seek amusement courting nightmares.

The Bookman

ABSALOM, ABSALOM!
WILLIAM FAULKNER
1936

From the first pages of this novel to the last we are con-
scious that the author is straining for strangeness. He
will say nothing simply. His paragraphs are so long and
so involved that it is hard to remember who is talking
or the subject which began the paragraph . . . We doubt
the story just as we doubt the conclusion . . . We do not
doubt the existence of decadence, but we do doubt that
it is the most important or the most interesting feature
in American life, or even Mississippi life.

Boston Evening Transcript

The final blowup of what was once a remarkable, if minor,
talent.

Clifton Fadiman, *The New Yorker*

TOM JONES
HENRY FIELDING
1749

A book seemingly intended to sap the foundation of that
morality which it is the duty of parents and all public
instructors to inculcate in the minds of young people.

Sir John Hawkins, *Life of Samuel Johnson*   1787

I scarcely know a more corrupt work.

> Samuel Johnson, quoted in *Memoirs*, Hannah More   1780

THE GREAT GATSBY
F. SCOTT FITZGERALD
1925

What has never been alive cannot very well go on living. So this is a book of the season only . . .

> *New York Herald Tribune*

A little slack, a little soft, more than a little artificial, *The Great Gatsby* falls into the class of negligible novels.

> *Springfield Republican*

Mr. F. Scott Fitzgerald deserves a good shaking . . . *The Great Gatsby* is an absurd story, whether considered as romance, melodrama, or plain record of New York high life.

> *Saturday Review of Literature*

TENDER IS THE NIGHT
F. SCOTT FITZGERALD
1934

Any second rate English society novelist could have written this story better than F. Scott Fitzgerald though not one could have touched his best chapters. Is it laziness, indifference, a lack of standards, or imperfect education that results in this constant botching of the first rate by American novelists?

Saturday Review of Literature

... none of the characters in this book is made sufficiently measurable at the beginning to give to his later downhill course anything more than mildly pathetic interest.

William Troy, *The Nation*

MADAME BOVARY
GUSTAVE FLAUBERT
1857

Monsieur Flaubert is not a writer.

Le Figaro

A PASSAGE TO INDIA
E.M. FORSTER
1924

Spiritually it is lacking in insight.

Blanche Watson, *The World Tomorrow*

MOSES AND MONOTHEISM
SIGMUND FREUD
1939

This book is poorly written, full of repetitions, replete with borrowings from unbelievers, and spoiled by the author's atheistic bias and his flimsy psycho-analytic fancies.

Catholic World

THE RECOGNITIONS
WILLIAM GADDIS
1955

The main fault of the novel is a complete lack of discipline ... It is a pity that, in his first novel, Gaddis did not have stronger editorial guidance than is apparent in the book, for he can write very well, even though most of the time he just lets his pen run on.

Kirkus Reviews

ON
EDWARD GIBBON

Gibbon's style is detestable; but is not the worst thing about him.

Samuel Taylor Coleridge, *Complete Works*　1853

Freud analyzes his reviewer.

WILHELM MEISTER
JOHANN WOLFGANG VON GOETHE
1829

Sheer nonsense.

Francis Jeffrey, *The Edinburgh Review*

THE RETURN OF THE NATIVE
THOMAS HARDY
1878

We maintain that the primary object of a story is to amuse us, and in the attempt to amuse us Mr. Hardy, in our opinion, breaks down.

Saturday Review

THE SCARLET LETTER
NATHANIEL HAWTHORNE
1850

Why has our author selected such a theme? . . . the nauseous amour of a Puritan pastor, with a frail creature of his charge, whose mind is represented as far more debauched than her body? Is it in short, because a running undertide of filth has become as requisite to a romance, as death in the fifth act of a tragedy? Is the French era actually begun in our literature?

Arthur Cleveland Coxe, *Church Review*

CATCH-22
JOSEPH HELLER
1961

Heller wallows in his own laughter and finally drowns in it. What remains is a debris of sour jokes, stage anger, dirty words, synthetic looniness, and the sort of antic behavior the children fall into when they know they are losing our attention.

Whitey Balliett, *The New Yorker*

There is a difference, after all, between milking a joke (the great gift of the old comedians) and stretching it out till you kill it. Mr. Heller has enough verve not to have to try so hard to be funny.

William Barrett, *Atlantic Monthly*

. . . it gasps for want of craft and sensibility . . . The book is an emotional hodgepodge; no mood is sustained long enough to register for more than a chapter.

New York Times Book Review

THE SUN ALSO RISES
ERNEST HEMINGWAY
1926

His characters are as shallow as the saucers in which they stack their daily emotions, and instead of interpreting his material—or even challenging it—he has been content merely to make a carbon copy of a not particularly significant surface life of Paris.

The Dial

. . . leaves one with the feeling that the people it describes really do not matter; one is left at the end with nothing to digest.

New York Times

FOR WHOM THE BELL TOLLS
ERNEST HEMINGWAY
1940

At a conservative estimate, one million dollars will be spent by American readers for this book. They will get for their money 34 pages of permanent value. These 34 pages tell of a massacre happening in a little Spanish town in the early days of the Civil War . . . Mr. Hemingway: please publish the massacre scene separately, and then forget *For Whom the Bell Tolls*; please leave stories of the Spanish Civil War to Malraux . . .

Commonweal

This book offers not pleasure but mounting pain; as literature it lacks the reserve that steadies genius and that lack not only dims its brilliance but makes it dangerous in its influence.

Catholic World

Hemingway edits for permanent value.

ON
HEMINGWAY

It is of course a commonplace that Hemingway lacks the serene confidence that he is a full-sized man.

Max Eastman, *New Republic* 1933

BRAVE NEW WORLD
ALDOUS HUXLEY
1932

A lugubrious and heavy-handed piece of propaganda.

New York Herald Tribune

. . . a somewhat amusing book; a bright man can do a good deal with two or three simple ideas.

Granville Hicks, *New Republic*

There are no surprises in it; and if he had no surprises to give us why should Mr. Huxley have bothered to turn this essay in indignation into a novel?

New Statesman and Nation

A DOLL'S HOUSE
HENRIK IBSEN

It was as though someone had dramatized the cooking of a Sunday dinner.

Clement Scott, *Sporting and Dramatic News* 1889

GHOSTS
HENRIK IBSEN
PERFORMED 1891, LONDON

The play performed last night is 'simple' enough in plan and purpose, but simple only in the sense of an open drain; of a loathsome sore unbandaged; of a dirty act done publicly.

Daily Telegram

ON
HENRY JAMES

It is becoming painfully evident that Mr. James has written himself out as far as the international novel is concerned, and probably as far as any kind of novel-writing is concerned.

William Morton Payne, *The Dial*   1884

(still to come from James were *The Bostonians*, *The Turn of the Screw*, *The Ambassadors* and others—Ed.)

James' denatured people are only the equivalent in fiction of those egg-faced, black-haired ladies who sit and sit in the Japanese colour-prints . . . These people cleared for artistic treatment never make lusty love, never go to angry war, never shout at an election or perspire at poker.

H.G. Wells, *Boon, The Mind of The Race, The Wild Asses of the Devil, and the Last Trump*   1915

. . . an idiot, and a Boston idiot, to boot, than which there is nothing lower in the world.

H.L. Mencken, *H.L. Mencken: The American Scene* 1965

DICTIONARY
SAMUEL JOHNSON
1755

I can assure the American public that the errors in Johnson's *Dictionary* are ten times as numerous as they suppose; and that the confidence now reposed in its accuracy is the greatest injury to philology that now exists.

Noah Webster, letter 1807

LIVES OF THE ENGLISH POETS
SAMUEL JOHNSON
1779-81

Johnson wrote the lives of the poets and left out the poets.

Elizabeth Barrett Browning, *The Book of the Poets* 1842

ON
SAMUEL JOHNSON

Insolent and loud, vain idol of a scribbling crowd . . . who, cursing flattery, is the tool of every fawning, flattering fool . . . Features so horrid, were it light, would put the devil himself to flight.

Charles Churchill, letter 1765

FROM HERE TO ETERNITY
JAMES JONES
1951

Certainly America has something better to offer the world, along with its arms and its armies, than such a confession of spiritual vacuum as this.

Christian Science Monitor

ULYSSES
JAMES JOYCE
1922

I finished Ulysses and think it is a misfire . . . The book is diffuse. It is brackish. It is pretentious. It is underbred, not only in the obvious but in the literary sense. A first rate writer, I mean, respects writing too much to be tricky.

Virginia Woolf, in her diary

That the book possesses literary importance, except as a tour de force, is hard to believe. If we are to have the literature of mere consciousness there are numerous examples from the later Henry James to Virginia Woolf

which import to consciousness a higher intrinsic value
and achieve the forms of art.

Springfield Republican reviewing the American
edition   1934

A PORTRAIT OF THE ARTIST AS A
YOUNG MAN
JAMES JOYCE
1917

. . . as a treatment of Irish politics, society or religion, it
is negligible.

Catholic World

FINNEGANS WAKE
JAMES JOYCE
1939

As one tortures one's way through *Finnegans Wake* an
impression grows that Joyce has lost his hold on human
life. Obsessed by a spaceless and timeless void, he has
outrun himself. We begin to feel that his very freedom
to say anything has become a compulsion to say nothing.

Alfred Kazin, *New York Herald Tribune*

ON
JOHN KEATS

John Keats's friends, we understand, destined him to the
career of medicine, and he was bound apprentice to a
worthy apothecary in town . . . It is a better and wiser

Mr. Keats chooses a profession.

thing to be a starved apothecary than a starved poet, so back to the shop, Mr. John, back to plasters, pills, and ointment boxes. But for heavens sake be a little more sparing of extenuatives and soporifics in your practice than you have been in your poetry.

Blackwood's Magazine   August, 1818

ON
RUDYARD KIPLING

I'm sorry, Mr. Kipling, but you just don't know how to use the English language.

San Francisco Examiner, rejection letter to Kipling   1889

DARKNESS AT NOON
ARTHUR KOESTLER
1941

The book is long, drawn out, full of repetitions, and marred throughout by its obscenity and irreligion.

Catholic World

ON
CHARLES LAMB

Charles Lamb I sincerely believe to be in some considerable degree insane. A more pitiful, rickety, gasping, staggering, Tomfool I do not know.

Thomas Carlyle, 1831, in *The Book of Insults*   1978

THE PLUMED SERPENT
D.H. LAWRENCE
1926

. . . if this writing up of a new faith is intended for a message, then it is only a paltry one, with its feathers, its bowls of human blood and its rhetoric.

The Spectator

LADY CHATTERLEY'S LOVER
D.H. LAWRENCE
1928

D. H. Lawrence has a diseased mind. He is obsessed by sex . . . we have no doubt that he will be ostracized by all except the most degenerate coteries in the literary world.

John Bull

MAIN STREET
SINCLAIR LEWIS
1920

It is full of the realism of fact colored by rather laborious and over clever satire. But it has no sustained action, whether as realism or as satire. It is a bulky collection of scenes, types, caricatures, humorous episodes, and facetious turns of phrase; a mine of comedy from which the ore has not been lifted.

The Weekly Review

BABBITT
SINCLAIR LEWIS
1922

As a humorist, Mr. Lewis makes valiant attempts to be funny; he merely succeeds in being silly. In fact it is as yellow a novel as novel can be.

Boston Evening Transcript

UNDER THE VOLCANO
MALCOLM LOWRY
1947

Mr. Lowry is passionately in earnest about what he has to say concerning human hope and defeat, but for all his earnestness he has succeeded only in writing a rather good imitation of an important novel.

The New Yorker

THE NAKED AND THE DEAD
NORMAN MAILER
1948

For the most part, the novel is a transcription of soldiers' talk, lusterless griping and ironed-out obscenities, too detailed and monotonous to have been imaginatively conceived for any larger purpose but too exact and literal to have been merely guessed at . . . This doesn't mean to

Mr. Lowry imitates an important novel.

deny Mailer his achievement. If he has a taste for transcribing banalities, he also has a talent for it.

New Republic

THE ASSISTANT
BERNARD MALAMUD
1957

Despite its occasional spark of humanity and its melancholy humor this is on the whole too grim a picture to have wide appeal.

Kirkus Reviews

BUDDENBROOKS
THOMAS MANN
1921

Very few Americans will take the trouble to read this book to the end. It contains no climaxes, no vivid surprises . . . Interesting as the story may be it is too loosely constructed, and for many readers that will prove a barrier.

Boston Evening Transcript

Nothing but two thick tomes in which the author describes the worthless story of worthless people in worthless chatter.

Eduard Engel, in *The Art of Folly*   1961

OF HUMAN BONDAGE
W. SOMERSET MAUGHAM
1935

Largely a record of sordid realism.

Athenaeum

Its ethics are frankly pagan.

The Independent

MOBY DICK
HERMAN MELVILLE
1851

. . . an ill-compounded mixture of romance and matter of fact . . . Mr. Melville has to thank himself only if his errors and his heroics are flung aside by the general reader as so much trash belonging to the worst school of Bedlam literature—since he seems not so much unable to learn as disdainful of learning the craft of an artist.

Athenaeum

Redburn was a stupid failure, *Mardi* was hopelessly dull, *White Jacket* was worse than either; and, in fact was such a very bad book, that, until the appearance of *Moby Dick* we had set it down as the very ultimatum of *weakness* to which the author could attain. It seems, however, that we were mistaken. In bombast, in caricature, in rhetorical artifice—generally as clumsy as it is ineffectual—and in low attempts at humor, each of his volumes has been an advance upon its predecessors.

Democratic Review

The captain's ravings and those of Mr. Melville are such as would justify a *writ de lunatico* against all parties.

Southern Quarterly Review

. . . a huge dose of hyperbolical slang, maudlin sentimentalism and tragic-comic bubble and squeak.

William Harrison Ainsworth, *New Monthly Magazine*

This sea novel is a singular medley of naval observation, magazine article writing, satiric reflection upon the conventionalisms of civilized life and rhapsody run mad . . .

The Spectator

PARADISE LOST
JOHN MILTON
1667

. . . do you not know that there is not perhaps *one page* in Milton's *Paradise Lost* in which he has not borrowed his imagry from the *scriptures*? I allow and rejoice that

Christ appealed only to the understanding and affections; but I affirm that after reading Isaiah, or St. Paul's *Epistle to The Hebrews*, Homer and Virgil are disgustingly *tame* to me and Milton himself barely tolerable.

Samuel Taylor Coleridge, *Letters* 1796

I could never read ten lines together without stumbling at some Pedantry that tipped me at once out of Paradise, or even Hell, into the schoolroom, worse than either.

Edward Fitzgerald, *Letters* 1876

LYCIDAS
JOHN MILTON
1638

The diction is harsh, the rhymes uncertain, and the numbers unpleasing . . . Its form is that of a pastoral—easy, vulgar and therefore disgusting.

Samuel Johnson, *Lives of The English Poets* 1779

ON
JOHN MILTON

His fame is gone out like a candle in a snuff and his memory will always stink.

William Winstanley, diary 1687

LOLITA
VLADIMIR NABOKOV
1958

That a book like this could be written—published here—sold, persumably over the counters, leaves one questioning the ethical and moral standards . . . there is a place for the exploration of abnormalities that does not lie in the public domain. Any librarian surely will question this for anything but the closed shelves. Any bookseller should be very sure that he knows in advance that he is selling very literate pornography.

Kirkus Reviews

MCTEAGUE
FRANK NORRIS
1899

. . . grossness for the sake of grossness . . . the world will not be proud of it in that distant tomorrow which irrevocably sets the true value on books of today.

The Literary World

WISE BLOOD
FLANNERY O'CONNOR
1952

A gloomy tale. The author tries to lighten it with humor, but unfortunately her idea of humor is almost exclusively variations on the pratfall . . . Neither satire nor humor is achieved.

Saturday Review of Literature

THE VIOLENT BEAR IT AWAY
FLANNERY O'CONNOR
1960

As a specialist in Southern horror stories, Miss O'Connor's attitude has been wry, her preferences perverse, her audience special.

Kirkus Reviews

APPOINTMENT IN SAMARRA
JOHN O'HARA
1934

There is a thorough-going vulgarity in this book, characteristic of its class, which is a symptom of a lack of knowledge of the novelist's real art . . . I mean an insufferable vulgarity, which has crept into so many of our supposedly advanced novels that someone not squeamish, not unread in earlier literatures, must protest against what is cheapening American fiction . . . What has happened to these young Americans? Do they think that living in a country the most vigorous, the most complex, the most problematical, the most interesting bar none in the world, we are going to be content with sour pap like this? And the tragedy is that they are clever; if they could see, they could write.

H.S. Canby, *Saturday Review of Literature*

MOURNING BECOMES ELECTRA
EUGENE O'NEILL
PERFORMED IN LONDON, 1961

Mourning Becomes Electra is hollow.

Bernard Levin, *Daily Express*

COMMON SENSE
THOMAS PAINE
1776

Shallow, violent and scurrilous.

William Edward Hartpole Lecky, *A History of England in the 18th Century* 1882

THE MOVIEGOER
WALKER PERCY
1961

Mr. Percy's prose needs oil and a good checkup.

The New Yorker

The New Yorker *repairs Mr. Percy's prose.*

THE BIRTHDAY PARTY
HAROLD PINTER

What all this means only Mr. Pinter knows, for as his characters speak in non sequiturs, half-gibberish and lunatic ravings, they are unable to explain their actions, thoughts or feelings. If the author can forget Beckett, Ionesco and Simpson he may do much better next time.

Manchester Guardian   1958

ON
EDGAR ALLAN POE

After reading some of Poe's stories one feels a kind of shock to one's modesty. We require some kind of spiritual ablution to cleanse our minds of his disgusting images.

Leslie Stephen, *Hours in A Library*   1874

A verbal poet merely; empty of thought, empty of sympathy, empty of love for any real thing . . . he was not human and manly.

John Burroughs, *The Dial*   1893

ON
EZRA POUND

A village explainer, excellent if you were a village, but if you were not, not.

Gertrude Stein, in *Dictionary of Biographical Quotation*   1978

REMEMBRANCE OF THINGS PAST
MARCEL PROUST
1913-1928

The sense of effort lies heavy over the whole work. That the book has greatness and passages of beauty redeeming its ugliness none will deny. But the mind demands of literature something that it can approve as well as something that it can enjoy; and in 'Cities of the Plain,' so full of dignitaries, so devoid of dignity, this instinct finds little to satisfy its craving.

> *Saturday Review of Literature* reviewing volume five of *Remembrance of Things Past*

My dear fellow, I may perhaps be dead from the neck up, but rack my brains as I may I can't see why a chap should need thirty pages to describe how he turns over in bed before going to sleep.

> Marc Humblot, French editor, rejection letter to Proust   1912

CALL IT SLEEP
HENRY ROTH
1935

The book lays all possible stress on the nastiness of the human animal. It is the fashion, and we must make the best of the spectacle of a fine book deliberately and as it were doggedly smeared with verbal filthiness.

> *New York Times Book Review*

M. Humblot contemplates turning over.

THE CATCHER IN THE RYE
J.D. SALINGER
1951

Recent war novels have accustomed us all to ugly words and images, but from the mouths of the very young and protected they sound peculiarly offensive . . . the ear refuses to believe.

New York Herald Tribune Book Review

THE HUMAN COMEDY
WILLIAM SAROYAN
1943

Alas! Interested though one is in the attempt, it remains to say that the result is not very happy . . . there is scarcely a trace of Saroyan's characteristic charm of manner, and indeed his art of inspired artlessness now falls extremely flat. This, in short, is an excessively simple and very, very sentimental little concoction.

Times Literary Supplement

KING LEAR
WILLIAM SHAKESPEARE
1605

This drama is chargeable with considerable imperfections.

Joseph Warton, *The Adventurer*   1754

HAMLET
WILLIAM SHAKESPEARE
1601

It is a vulgar and barbarous drama, which would not be tolerated by the vilest populace of France, or Italy . . . one would imagine this piece to be the work of a drunken savage.

> Voltaire, (1768), in *The Works of M. de Voltaire* 1901

OTHELLO
WILLIAM SHAKESPEARE
1604

Pure melodrama. There is not a touch of characterization that goes below the skin.

> George Bernard Shaw, *Saturday Review* 1897

ANTONY AND CLEOPATRA
WILLIAM SHAKESPEARE
1606

To say that there is plenty of bogus characterization in it . . . is merely to say that it is by Shakespeare.

> George Bernard Shaw, *Saturday Review* 1897

JULIUS CAESAR
WILLIAM SHAKESPEARE
PERFORMED IN LONDON, 1898

There is not a single sentence uttered by Shakespeare's Julius Caesar that is, I will not say worthy of him, but worthy of an average Tammany boss.

George Bernard Shaw, *Saturday Review*

ROMEO AND JULIET
WILLIAM SHAKESPEARE
PERFORMED IN LONDON, 1662

March 1st—To the Opera and there saw Romeo and Juliet, the first time it was ever acted; but it is a play of itself the worst that ever I heard in my life, and the worst acted that ever I saw these people do. . . .

Samuel Pepys, *Diary*

A MIDSUMMER NIGHT'S DREAM
WILLIAM SHAKESPEARE
PERFORMED IN LONDON, 1662

The most insipid, ridiculous play that I ever saw in my life.

Samuel Pepys, *Diary*

ON
WILLIAM SHAKESPEARE

Shakespeare's name, you may depend on it, stands absurdly too high and will go down. He had no invention as to stories, none whatever. He took all his plots from old novels, and threw their stories into a dramatic shape, at as little expense of thought as you or I could turn his plays back again into prose tales.

Lord Byron, letter to James Hogg   1814

ARMS AND THE MAN
GEORGE BERNARD SHAW
PERFORMED IN LONDON, 1894

Shaw may one day write a serious and even an artistic play, if he will only repress his irreverent whimsicality, try to clothe his character conceptions in flesh and blood, and realize the difference between knowingness and knowledge.

William Archer, *World*

MAJOR BARBARA
GEORGE BERNARD SHAW
PERFORMED IN LONDON, 1905

There are no human beings in *Major Barbara:* only animated points of view.

William Archer, *World*

MAN AND SUPERMAN
GEORGE BERNARD SHAW
PERFORMED IN LONDON, 1904

I think Shaw, on the whole, is more bounder than genius ... I couldn't get on with *Man and Superman:* it disgusted me.

Bertrand Russell, letter to G.L. Dickinson

PROMETHEUS UNBOUND
PERCY BYSSHE SHELLEY
1819

... absolute raving ... his principles are ludicrously wicked, and his poetry a melange of nonsense, cockneyism, poverty and pedantry.

Literary Gazette

THE JUNGLE
UPTON SINCLAIR
1906

His reasoning is so false, his disregard of human nature so naive, his statement of facts so biased, his conclusions so perverted, that the effect can be only to disgust many honest, sensible folk with the very terms he uses so glibly.

The Bookman

THE FAERIE QUEENE
EDMUND SPENSER
1590-96

The tediousness of continued allegory, and that too seldom striking or ingenious, has also contributed to render the Fairy Queen peculiarly tiresome ... Spenser maintains his place upon the shelves, among our English classics; but he is seldom seen on the table.

David Hume, in *The History of Great Britain*   1759

ON
GERTRUDE STEIN

It's a shame you never knew her before she went to pot. You know a funny thing, she never could write dialogue. It was terrible. She learned how to do it from my stuff ... She never could forgive learning that and she was afraid people would notice it, where she'd learned it, so she had to attack me. It's a funny racket, really. But I swear she was damned nice before she got ambitious.

Ernest Hemingway, in *Green Hills of Africa*   1935

OF MICE AND MEN
JOHN STEINBECK
1937

An oxymoronic combination of the tough and tender, *Of Mice and Men* will appeal to sentimental cynics, cyn-

Mr. Hume struck by an allegory.

ical sentimentalists . . . Readers less easily thrown off their trolley will still prefer Hans Andersen.

Time

LIE DOWN IN DARKNESS
WILLIAM STYRON
1951

What is evident in this first novel is an eagerness and a sincerity which ought to have been served by an able and understanding editor. Mr. Styron however had no Maxwell Perkins to guide him, with the result that he has written here a serious work of fiction which should not have exceeded 300 pages in length, and which need not have been done in so turgid and often confused a manner . . . Mr. Styron leaves his readers curiously unsympathetic.

August Perleth, *Chicago Tribune*

GULLIVER'S TRAVELS
JONATHAN SWIFT
1726

. . . evidence of a diseased mind and lacerated heart.

John Dunlop, *The History of Fiction* 1814

A counsel of despair.

George A. Aitken, *Gulliver's Travels*   1896

WALDEN
HENRY DAVID THOREAU
1854

I look upon a great deal of the modern sentimentalism about Nature as a mark of disease. It is one more symptom of the general liver complaint . . . (Thoreau's) shanty life was a mere impossibility so far as his own conception of it goes, as an entire independency of mankind. He squatted on another man's land; he borrows his axe; his boards, his nails, his fish hooks, his plough, his hoe—all turn state's evidence against him as an accomplice in the sin of that artificial civilization which rendered it possible that such a person as Henry David Thoreau should exist at all.

James Russell Lowell, 1865, from *Literary Essays*   1890

ANNA KARENINA
LEO TOLSTOI
1877

Sentimental rubbish . . . Show me one page that contains an idea.

The Odessa Courier

THE ADVENTURES OF HUCKLEBERRY FINN
MARK TWAIN
1884

A gross trifling with every fine feeling . . . Mr. Clemens has no reliable sense of propriety.

Springfield Republican

ON
MARK TWAIN

A hundred years from now it is very likely that 'The Jumping Frog' alone will be remembered.

Harry Thurston Peck, *The Bookman*   1901

RABBIT RUN
JOHN UPDIKE
1960

This grim little story is told with all the art we have learned to expect from Updike, but the nagging question remains: what does it come to? Rabbit, Janice and Ruth are all creatures of instinct, floundering in a world they cannot understand . . . The author fails to convince us that his puppets are interesting in themselves or that their plight has implications that transcend their narrow world.

Milton Crane, *Chicago Tribune*

CANDIDE
VOLTAIRE
1759

It seems to have been written by a creature of a nature wholly different from our own, indifferent to our lot, rejoicing in our sufferings, and laughing like a demon or an ape at the misery of this human race with which he has nothing in common.

Mme de Staël, *De L'Allemagne*

ALL THE KING'S MEN
ROBERT PENN WARREN
1946

Somewhere, Mr. Warren loses his grip on his backwoods opportunities and becomes so absorbed in a number of other characters that what might have been a useful study of an irresponsible politician whose prototype we have had melancholy occasion to observe in the flesh turns out to be a disappointment.

The New Yorker

The language of both men and women is coarse, blasphemous and revolting—their actions would shame a pagan hottentot.

Catholic World

VILE BODIES
EVELYN WAUGH
1930

Mr. Waugh displays none of the élan that distinguishes the true satirist from the caricaturist. For all its brilliance the writing lacks vitality. The invention is tired, and effects are too often got by recourse to the devices of slapstick exaggeration.

Dudley Fitts, *The Nation*

MISS LONELYHEARTS
NATHANAEL WEST
1933

A knowledge of its contents will be essential to conversational poise in contemporary literature during the next three months—perhaps.

Boston Evening Transcript

LEAVES OF GRASS
WALT WHITMAN
1855

No, no, this kind of thing won't do . . . The good folks down below (I mean posterity) will have none of it.

James Russell Lowell, quoted in *The Complete Works*, Vol. 14   1904

Whitman is as unacquainted with art as a hog is with mathematics.

The London Critic

Of course, to call it poetry, in any sense, would be mere abuse of language.

William Allingham, letter to W.M. Rossetti   1857

DRUM-TAPS
WALT WHITMAN
1865

Mr. Whitman's attitude seems monstrous. It is monstrous because it pretends to persuade the soul while it slights the intellect; because it pretends to gratify the feelings while it outrages the taste . . . Our hearts are often touched through a compromise with the artistic sense but never in direct violation of it.

Henry James, *The Nation*

ON
WALT WHITMAN

Incapable of true poetical originality, Whitman had the cleverness to invent a literary trick, and the shrewdness to stick to it.

Peter Bayne, *Contemporary Review*   1875

Whitman instructs hog.

Whitman, like a large shaggy dog, just unchained, scouring the beaches of the world and baying at the moon.

Robert Louis Stevenson, *Familiar Studies* 1882

. . . his lack of a sense of poetic fitness, his failure to understand the business of a poet, is clearly astounding.

Francis Fisher Browne, *The Dial* 1882

He was a vagabond, a reprobate, and his poems contain outbursts of erotomania so artlessly shameless that their parallel in literature could hardly be found with the author's name attached. For his fame he has to thank just those bestially sensual pieces which first drew him to the attention of all the pruriency of America. He is morally insane, and incapable of distinguishing between good and evil, virtue and crime.

Max Nordau, *Degeneration* 1895

THE PICTURE OF
DORIAN GRAY
OSCAR WILDE
1891

. . . unmanly, sickening, vicious (though not exactly what is called 'improper'), and tedious.

Athenaeum

LOOK HOMEWARD, ANGEL
THOMAS WOLFE
1929

It seems to be the great gift of Mr. Wolfe that everything is interesting, valuable, and significant to him. It must be confessed that he has just missed the greatest of gifts, that of being able to convey his interest to the ordinary reader.

Basil Davenport, *Saturday Review of Literature*

TO THE LIGHTHOUSE
VIRGINIA WOOLF
1927

Her work is poetry; it must be judged as poetry, and all the weaknesses of poetry are inherent in it.

New York Evening Post

THE WAVES
VIRGINIA WOOLF
1931

This chamber music, this closet fiction, is executed behind too firmly closed windows . . . The book is dull.

H.C. Harwood, *Saturday Review of Literature*

THE PRELUDE
WILLIAM WORDSWORTH
1850

The story is the old story. There are the old raptures about mountains and cataracts. The old flimsy philosophy about the effect of scenery on the mind; the old crazy mystical metaphysics; the endless wilderness of dull, flat, prosaic twaddle . . ."

T.B. Macaulay, in his journal

NATIVE SON
RICHARD WRIGHT
1940

The astounding thing is that the publisher is able to send out with the book a typescript about the weight of a Tor Bay Sole entirely made up of favorable reviews from the American Press. Over here and away from that particular racial problem the book seems unimpressive and silly, not even as much fun as a thriller.

New Statesman and Nation

II

ROTTEN REVIEWS

CONTEMPORARY NASTINESS

Selecting bad blurbs for the previous portion of this volume was rather simple. Certain books had come to be regarded as classics and all of these books had been bitterly resented at some time by reviewers.

Choosing contemporary titles to be represented here has not been easy. We do not have history to tell us what has endured. Instead we asked selected authors to contribute their favorite critic's snarls. Many did, with delight, and thus these authors had the last laugh, if not the last word, on their detractors.

We also scouted around for the really bitter blast—the review that is so malicious that it trips over itself.

Finally, we picked books and authors that remain a force in our time—even though enduring a decade is not an especially remarkable feat when compared to the staying power of the classics.

One of the delights in compiling this selection was the chance to hear from many authors with their opinions about the whole review process. Portions of their letters to Pushcart are included later.

We expect that many of our readers will be examining this volume in a secluded, small room (see Ansel Adams' letter to Wallace Stegner) and we think this is appropriate.

BILL HENDERSON

THE MONKEY WRENCH GANG
EDWARD ABBEY
1975

The author of this book should be neutered and locked away forever.

San Juan County Record

ABBEY'S ROAD
EDWARD ABBEY
1978

If you want to read 200 pages of Edward Abbey's self-flattery buy this . . . smug, graceless book.

The New Republic

COUNTING THE WAYS
EDWARD ALBEE
1977

. . . the play sounds like George Burns and Gracie Allen trying to keep up a dinner conversation with Wittgenstein . . . I have never seen such desperately ingratiating smiles on the faces of actors.

Newsweek

A WALK ON THE WILD SIDE
NELSON ALGREN
1956

. . . my, how this boy needs editing!

San Francisco Chronicle

ONE FAT ENGLISHMAN
KINGSLEY AMIS
1964

. . . fatty is not only a boor, but a bore, and that quickly makes the satire a matter of satiety.

America

THE HANDMAID'S TALE
MARGARET ATWOOD
1986

Norman Mailer, wheezing lewd approval of some graphic images he encountered in the writing of Germaine Greer, remarked that 'a wind in this prose whistled up the kilt of male conceit.' Reading Margaret Atwood, I don my kilt but the wind never comes. Just a cold breeze.

The American Spectator

Reader checks reviewer's kilt.

GIOVANNI'S ROOM
JAMES BALDWIN
1956

No matter of careful recording of detail or of poetic heightening of feeling can supply what is absent here—the understanding which is vital whether a character in fiction merely takes a walk or commits incest . . .

Commonweal

THE SOTWEED FACTOR
JOHN BARTH
1961

. . . too long, too long, too long.

New York Herald Tribune

GILES GOAT-BOY
JOHN BARTH
1966

. . . a pervasive silliness that turns finally—if one must bring up the university image—into college humor, a kind of MAD magazine joke.

Christian Science Monitor

LOVE ALWAYS
ANN BEATTIE
1985

. . . Beattie's admirable eye for the telling detail has unfortunately developed a squint . . .

Commonweal

HOW IT IS
SAMUEL BECKETT
1964

. . . he breeds nothing but confusion. His plays and novels present a vision of life that is shockingly unchristian. They make the life and death of our Lord just one more of the legends man has used to delude himself . . . Beckett is postulating this as our inescapable condition of life. It may be for him. Not for this reader.

R.H. Glauber, *Christian Century*

THE ADVENTURES OF AUGIE MARCH
SAUL BELLOW
1953

All of Those Words, in denominations of from three to five letters, are present.

Library Journal

HENDERSON THE RAIN KING
SAUL BELLOW
1959

The novelist who doesn't like meanings writes an allegory; the allegory means that men should not mean but be. Ods bodkins. The reviewer looks at the evidence and wonders if he should damn the author and praise the book, or praise the author and damn the book. And is it possible, somehow or other to praise or damn, both? He isn't sure.

Reed Whittemore, *New Republic*

At times Henderson is too greyly overcast with thought to be more than a dun Quixote.

Time

HERZOG
SAUL BELLOW
1961

There is no effort toward decency—many of the conversations that come back to Herzog are foul-mouthed, and his own sexual actions and reminiscences are unrestrained.

America

LITTLE BIG MAN
THOMAS BERGER
1964

. . . a farce that is continually over-reaching itself. Or, as the Cheyenne might put it, Little Big Man Little Overblown.

Gerald Walker, *New York Times Book Review*

THE MAN WHO KNEW KENNEDY
VANCE BOURJAILY
1967

The man who knew Kennedy didn't know him very well. I'm almost as intimate with Lyndon Johnson. I met him once.

Webster Schott, *New York Times Book Review*

WOMEN AND ANGELS
HAROLD BRODKEY
1985

. . . much of it reads like an extended obituary produced by a team of more than usually fanciful computers.

New York Review of Books

A CLOCKWORK ORANGE
ANTHONY BURGESS
1963

. . . 'The holy bearded veck all nagoy hanging on a cross'
is an example of the author's language and questionable
taste. . . . The author seems content to use a serious social
challenge for frivolous purposes, but himself to stay
neutral.

Times (London)

THE TICKET THAT EXPLODED
WILLIAM BURROUGHS
1967

The works of William Burroughs . . . have been taken
seriously, even solemnly, by some literary types, including Mary McCarthy and Norman Mailer. Actually, Burroughs's work adds up to the world's pluperfect put-on.

Time

NAKED LUNCH
WILLIAM BURROUGHS
1963

. . . the merest trash, not worth a second look.

New Republic

NOVA EXPRESS
WILLIAM BURROUGHS
1964

. . . The book is unnecessary.

Granville Hicks, *Saturday Review*

IN COLD BLOOD
TRUMAN CAPOTE
1965

One can say of this book—with sufficient truth to make it worth saying: 'This isn't writing. It's research.'

Stanley Kauffmann, *The New Republic*

WHAT WE TALK ABOUT WHEN WE TALK ABOUT LOVE
RAYMOND CARVER
1980

There is nothing here to appease a reader's basic literary needs.

Atlantic Monthly

CASTLE TO CASTLE
LOUIS FERDINAND CÉLINE
1969

. . . quite a tedious book.

John Weightman, *New York Review of Books*

THE WAPSHOT SCANDAL
JOHN CHEEVER
1964

Fatally flawed.

Hilary Corke, *New Republic*

WHAT THE LIGHT WAS LIKE
AMY CLAMPITT
1985

. . . it would be better for Amy Clampitt if, at least for a while, she tucked her notes from Poetry 101 away in a trunk.

Poetry

MRS. BRIDGE
EVAN CONNELL
1959

It's hard to believe that a lady from Kansas City with a house in the best residential section, one full-time maid, one mink coat and a Lincoln for her very own, should finish up as timorous and ephemeral as a lunar moth on the outside of a window.

Florence Crowther, *New York Times Book Review*

NOTES FROM A BOTTLE FOUND ON THE BEACH AT CARMEL
EVAN CONNELL
1963

. . . almost pure gingerbread. It has bite, a certain flavor, but it turns into a gluey mass when chewed.

San Francisco Examiner

MR. BRIDGE
EVAN CONNELL
1969

It is hard to imagine a creep like Bridge ever lived. If he did, so what? Connell fails to show that he has any relevance to what's happening in America, 1969.

Cleveland Press

A novel should be something more than an X-ray of a dull life.

Bridgeport Post

SON OF MORNING STAR
EVAN CONNELL
1985

Unfortunately, the big story often seems to elude Connell, who is obsessed with digression, flashback and flashforward.

Commentary

This do-it-yourself kit will appeal to those who think confusion is a narrative strategy.

J.O. Tate, *National Review*

THE ORIGIN OF THE BRUNISTS
ROBERT COOVER
1966

. . . an explosion in a cesspool.

Bruno McAndrew, *Best Sellers*

THE PUBLIC BURNING
ROBERT COOVER
1977

. . . an overwritten bore . . . a protracted sneer.

Paul Gray, *Time*

GERALD'S PARTY
ROBERT COOVER
1986

The Novel should develop a reader's sensitivities, not deaden them with risible comic-strip.

New Statesman

SALVADOR
JOAN DIDION
1983

. . . she makes the tiny republic of El Salvador into a mirror reflecting her own basic contempt for liberal democracy and—why not say it?—the American Way of Life.

Commentary

PILGRIM AT TINKER CREEK
ANNIE DILLARD
1974

I have never seen frogs in Virginia 'shout and glare' . . .

Loren Eiseley, *Washington Post Book World*

THE GINGER MAN
J.P. DONLEAVY
1958

Disgust, indignation, and boredom—those are the most likely responses to be anticipated among readers of *The Ginger Man*. No doubt the book will also get a few screams of praise from those who habitually confuse the effects of art with the effects of shock and sensation . . . This rather nasty, rather pompous novel gives us, in all, a precocious small boy's view of life, the boy having been spoiled somehow and allowed to indulge in sulks and tantrums and abundant self-pity.

Chicago Tribune

10:30 ON A SUMMER NIGHT
MARGUERITE DURAS
1963

. . . has the proud air of saying in her every painful, glottal line, 'Hup for prose!'

Hortense Calisher, *The Nation*

INVISIBLE MAN
RALPH ELLISON
1952

It has its faults which cannot simply be shrugged off—occasional overwriting, stretches of fuzzy thinking, and a tendency to waver, confusingly, between realism and surrealism.

Atlantic Monthly

A FAN'S NOTES
FREDERICK EXLEY
1968

The book's fault is its lack of passion.

Library Journal

LOVE AND DEATH IN THE AMERICAN NOVEL
LESLIE FIEDLER
1960

The author can't win, ever, by Fiedler's standard of judgment. Only the critic can win. . . . There is more in American fiction, much more, than Fiedler has been able to find.

Malcolm Cowley, *New York Times Book Review*

THE FEMININE MYSTIQUE
BETTY FRIEDAN
1963

...It is a pity that Mrs. Friedan has to fight so hard to persuade herself as well as her readers of her argument. In fact her passion against the forces of the irrational in life quite carries her away.

Yale Review

It is superficial to blame the 'culture' and its handmaidens, the women's magazines, as she does ... To paraphrase a famous line, 'the fault dear Mrs. Friedan, is not in our culture, but in ourselves.'

New York Times Book Review

ON ROBERT FROST

If it were thought that anything I wrote was influenced by Robert Frost, I would take that particular work of mine, shred it, and flush it down the toilet, hoping not to clog the pipes.

James Dickey

THE RECOGNITIONS
WILLIAM GADDIS
1955

The Recognitions is an evil book, a scurrilous book, a profane book, a scatological book and an exasperating book...what this squalling overwritten book needs above all is to have its mouth washed out with lye soap. It reeks of decay and filth and perversion and half digested learning.

Chicago Sun Times

JR
WILLIAM GADDIS
1976

To produce an unreadable text, to sustain this foxy purpose over 726 pages, demands rare powers. Mr William Gaddis has them.

George Steiner, *The New Yorker*

(Gaddis) dumps everything into these pages except what they most desperately need—the ironic and flexible detachment of a discriminating mind.

Pearl K. Bell, *The New Leader*

OLT

KENNETH GANGEMI

1970

Really the most interesting part is the jacket information that Gangemi was born in Scarsdale, took an engineering degree at R.P.I....

William Pritchard, *Hudson Review*

ON DORIS GRUMBACH

On television I see Mary McCarthy talking about her Vassar friend, the poet Elizabeth Bishop. I notice Mary's instant icy smile, so often present when I interviewed her in Paris in 1966 for a book. George Grosz saw the same smile on Lenin's face. "It doesn't mean a smile," he said. I am fascinated by it. It represents, I think, an unsuccessful attempt to soften a harsh, bluntly stated judgement. Last summer, twenty-two years after the book I wrote about her, which she so disliked, appeared, I encountered Mary for the first time in an outdoor market in Blue Hill.

"Hello, Mary," I said. "Do you remember me?"

Her smile flashed and then, like a worn-out bulb, disappeared instantly.

"Unfortunately," she said.

It didn't mean a smile.

Doris Grumbach

MICKELSSON'S GHOSTS
JOHN GARDNER
1982

. . . dreadfully long and padded and it often degenerates into drivel . . . as a philosophical novel, it is a sham. Stripped of its excesses, however, it does not have enough substance to have made a good Raymond Carver short story.

Saturday Review

THE WRECKAGE OF AGATHON
JOHN GARDNER
1970

'Wreckage' is appropriate . . . more hysterical than historical.

Library Journal

OCTOBER LIGHT
JOHN GARDNER
1977

Within this great welter of words, symbols and gassy speechifying and half-hatched allegory there was once, I suspect, a good lean novel, but I can't find it . . .

Peter Prescott, *Newsweek*

OMENSETTER'S LUCK
WILLIAM H. GASS
1966

. . . Gass has not a particle of the savoir-faire of Faulkner. The pages ramble on, almost devoid of dialogue. This first novel is not for the reader longing for a good story narrative.

Library Journal

IN THE HEART OF THE
HEART OF THE COUNTRY
WILLIAM H. GASS
1968

The publisher promises that anyone who has a deep love for the well-made English sentence will find these stories richly rewarding. Perhaps so. But there is every chance that the rest of us—those who prefer to curl up with a good book—will be left gasping with boredom instead.

Book World

HOWL AND OTHER POEMS
ALLEN GINSBERG
1956

It is only fair to Allen Ginsberg . . . to remark on the utter lack of decorum of any kind in his dreadful little volume . . . 'Howl' is meant to be a noun, but I can't help taking it as an imperative.

John Hollander, *Partisan Review*

THE PERFECTIONISTS
GAIL GODWIN
1971

. . . the men are all fatuous and self-centered creatures. This is then a woman's novel in a narrow and constricting way.

Saturday Review

THE ODD WOMAN
GAIL GODWIN
1974

A generous, sensitive, intelligent, humane and literate book that despite its generosity, sensitivity, humanity, and literacy, manages to be a deadly bore.

The New Yorker

A MOTHER AND TWO DAUGHTERS
GAIL GODWIN
1981

Godwin earnestly sticks by her characters . . . The only
trouble is, like the people next door, they're nice but not
very interesting.

Saturday Review

LORD OF THE FLIES
WILLIAM GOLDING
1955

. . . completely unpleasant.

The New Yorker

GROWING UP ABSURD
PAUL GOODMAN
1961

The worst written book I have read in quite a long time.

D.W. Brogan, *The Guardian*

THE TIN DRUM
GÜNTER GRASS
1963

Bewildered by the torrent of fantastic incident, mystified by what Günter Grass intends by it all, one feels like a zoologist who discovers some monstrous unrecorded mammal gobbling leaves: It may have beautiful horns, but what is it?

New Statesman

THE FEMALE EUNUCH
GERMAINE GREER
1971

Bores aid no revolution.

Library Journal

WEBSTER'S THIRD NEW INTERNATIONAL DICTIONARY OF THE ENGLISH LANGUAGE
PHILIP BABCOCK GROVE, EDITOR
1962

. . . a copyeditor's despair, a propounder of endless riddles.

Atlantic Monthly

WE BOMBED IN NEW HAVEN
JOSEPH HELLER
1968

A dud of the first magnitude . . .

Saturday Review

SOMETHING HAPPENED
JOSEPH HELLER
1974

. . . surely it's time to declare a moratorium on brain-damaged children used as metaphors for mental and emotional decay.

Library Journal

GOOD AS GOLD
JOSEPH HELLER
1979

. . . a self-indulgent ventilation of private spleen . . . Heller operates as if he were a jewel thief wearing boxing gloves.

Newsweek

TOYS IN THE ATTIC
LILLIAN HELLMAN
1961

It is curious how incest, impotence, nymphomania, religious mania and real estate speculation can be so dull.

Richard Findlater, *Time and Tide*

Lillian Hellman has chosen to write on a Tennessee Williams theme in an Agatha Christie style.

Times (London)

SCOUNDREL TIME
LILLIAN HELLMAN
1977

Scoundrel Time is historically a fraud, artistically a put-up job and emotionally packed with meanness.

Dwight MacDonald, *Esquire*

A MOVEABLE FEAST
ERNEST HEMINGWAY
1964

Judging by this memoir, it would seem the Hemingway estate is prepared to dribble out some very small beer indeed in the name of the master. This book was appar-

ently completed in Cuba in 1960 and, for all the good it
is likely to do Hemingway's reputation, it could very well
have stayed there—permanently . . .

Geoffrey Wagner, *Commonweal*

CAT MAN
EDWARD HOAGLAND
1956

This lengthy description of the lower depths of existence
among men who pick up a living around travelling cir-
cuses is frequently disgusting in an eager, repetitious,
small-boy way.

The New Yorker

THE DEPUTY
ROLF HOCHHUTH
1964

The Deputy on Broadway is like one of those comic-strip
versions of a literary classic . . . and as the characters
bestride the stage you can virtually see the balloons com-
ing out of their mouths.

John Simon, *Hudson Review*

POEMS 1934-1969
DAVID IGNATOW
1970

Milch-poems I'd call them, reliable for uniform milk.

Chicago Tribune

NEW AND COLLECTED POEMS: 1970-1985
DAVID IGNATOW
1986

A reader prone to despondency had better steel himself before encountering David Ignatow's poems—or avoid them, unless he believes in homeopathy.

Poetry

THE HOTEL NEW HAMPSHIRE
JOHN IRVING
1981

Eager to reassure us that his novel is all in good fun despite the bloody goings-on, Irving resorts to a gee-whiz idiom right out of 'Leave It To Beaver.'

James Atlas, *New York Times Book Review*

Dave Ignatow had a farm...

... not only a confusing but a boring novel ... John Irving ought to quit wasting his time ...

The Nation

FEAR OF FLYING
ERICA JONG
1974

This crappy novel, misusing vulgarity to the point where it becomes purely foolish, picturing women as a hapless organ animated by the simplest ridicule, and devaluing imagination in every line ... represents everything that is to be loathed in American fiction today.

Paul Theroux, *New Statesman*

LEGS
WILLIAM KENNEDY
1975

... a made for TV book. Consult your local listings for time and station.

Library Journal

CONTEMPORARIES
ALFRED KAZIN
1962

This critic is a man who knows all there is to know about literature except how to enjoy it ...

Nelson Algren, *The Nation*

ON THE ROAD
JACK KEROUAC
1957

He can slip from magniloquent hysteria into sentimental bathos, and at his worst he merely slobbers words . . . a writer to watch, but if this watching is to be rewarded, he must begin to watch himself.

Chicago Tribune

ONE FLEW OVER THE CUCKOO'S NEST
KEN KESEY
1962

Kesey builds up an atmosphere of real horror and significance and then dispels it ineffectively with some quite misplaced slapstick. The book never gets back firmly on the track and a flurry of activity at the end isn't quite lively enough to disguise the fact that it's getting nowhere.

Commonweal

THE WHITE HOUSE YEARS
HENRY KISSINGER
1979

Doctor Henry Kissinger has constructed a diplomacy for a Hobbesian world . . . When he exercised that diplo-

macy he helped create the kind of world that would justify it.

New Republic

MIDNIGHT WAS MY CRY
CAROLYN KIZER
1971

Like most poets, she teaches, and like most teachers, she
isn't very good.

Esquire

THE GOLDEN NOTEBOOK
DORIS LESSING
1962

The novel is a ponderous bore.

Julian Mitchell, *The Spectator*

Few readers will want to subject themselves to the
demands of this huge complex and ugly book . . . The
apparatus becomes tiresome, the obscenities and clinical
language depressing; the occasional satisfactions of seeing
how bits of the puzzle fit together are not enough.

Christian Science Monitor

ADVERTISEMENT FOR MYSELF
NORMAN MAILER
1960

The book as a whole shapes up as a manifesto of a writer on his way out. . . . The plain fact is that, soured by what he interprets as 'defeat' at the hands of 'a most loathsome literary world, necrophilic to the core,' Mailer has chosen to be a literary terrorist.

Atlantic Monthly

. . . a record of an artistic crackup.

Time

AN AMERICAN DREAM
NORMAN MAILER
1965

Mailer meant to make money with this book. Hollywood should go for it. It should make the Best Seller lists. But it is a book calculated to leave All America holding its nose.

Best Sellers

Not for a moment can the novel be taken seriously as a portrayal of life in America—or anywhere else . . . I should like to believe the novel is a hoax.

Granville Hicks, *Saturday Review*

WHY ARE WE IN VIETNAM?
NORMAN MAILER
1967

. . . a third rate work of art, but it's a first rate outrage to our sensibilities.

Anatole Broyard, *New York Times Book Review*

THE GROUP
MARY MCCARTHY
1963

The McCarthy lode is petering out.

America

. . . a minor achievement and a major disappointment.

Stanley Kauffmann, *New Republic*

BIRDS OF AMERICA
MARY MCCARTHY
1971

. . . a weight watcher's erotic dream and Miss McCarthy's most saporific fiction yet.

Peter Prescott, *Newsweek*

"UNDERGROUND"
THOMAS MCGRATH
1986

. . . barbaric yawps.

Kirkus Reviews

TROPIC OF CAPRICORN
HENRY MILLER
1962
FIRST PUBLISHED IN PARIS, 1939

. . . a flamboyant failure.

San Francisco Chronicle

. . . a gadfly with delusions of grandeur.

Time

TAR BABY
TONI MORRISON
1981

Heavy-handed, and ultimately unintelligible. . . topples into dreadful pits of bombast.

The New Yorker

THE AMERICAN WAY OF DEATH
JESSICA MITFORD
1963

While hiding behind the commercial aspects of the mortician and the cemeteries and mausoleums where our

Congressman hunts Commies.

dear departed friends and relatives are commemorated, she is really striking another blow at the Christian religion. Her tirade against morticians is simply the vehicle to carry her anti-Christ attack . . . I would rather place my mortal remains, alive or dead, in the hands of any American mortician than to set foot on the soil of any Communist nation.

Congressman James B. Utt, *Congressional Record*

PALE FIRE
VLADIMIR NABOKOV
1962

Perhaps for some tastes the verbal display and the internal trickery will be sufficient to outweigh the uncleanness that almost seems to stick to the reader's hands. Others, like this reader, may consider *Pale Fire* a prodigal waste of its author's gifts.

Roderick Nordell, *Christian Science Monitor*

A HOUSE FOR MR. BISWAS
V.S. NAIPAUL
1962

Naipaul's House, though built of excellent exotic materials, sags badly; economy, style, and a less elastic blueprint would have done wonders.

Time

THE OAK IN THE ACORN
HOWARD NEMEROV
1987

... fairly feeble attempt to explain Proust ... an unilluminating exercise in Marcel-worship.

Kirkus Reviews

THEM
JOYCE CAROL OATES
1969

... earnestly out of it ... her version of what people feel now in the inner city in riot areas is as naive as a proto-Martian's might be.

Library Journal

ON BOXING
JOYCE CAROL OATES
1987

Clearly this represents an attempt by a purely feminine psyche to come to terms with the purely masculine ... While she touches the metaphysical soul of boxing, it is questionable whether she ever lays a glove on its heart ... real men need more blood and guts.

Allen Fletcher, *Worcester Sunday Telegram*

SERMONS AND SODA-WATER
JOHN O'HARA
1960

The novellas represent no change in Mr. O'Hara's method. He normally puts everything into a novel, including the kitchen sink complete with stopped drain, plumber, and plumber's mate, and does this not once but four or five times per book. The novella form has merely limited the author in a statistical way; one kitchen sink is all he can fit into his predetermined space . . .

Atlantic Monthly

THE BIG LAUGH
JOHN O'HARA
1962

When O'Hara is good he is very, very good; when he is bad he is writing for Hollywood . . . an exercise in tedium.

New York Herald Tribune

THE HORSE KNOWS THE WAY
JOHN O'HARA
1964

One might suggest . . . that the inhabitants of hell be condemned to an eternity reading stories behind the headlines in American tabloids . . . John O'Hara's new collection of short stories brings the whole realm uncomfortably close. It is a punishment to read . . .

Christian Science Monitor

LOOK BACK IN ANGER
JOHN OSBORNE
1956

. . . sets up a wailing wall for the latest post-war generation of under-thirties. It aims at being a despairing cry but achieves only the stature of a self-pitying snivel.

Evening Standard

INADMISSIBLE EVIDENCE
JOHN OSBORNE
1964

Before the end a feeling obtrudes that a bulldozer is being used where a trowel would have done.

Philip Hope-Wallace, *The Guardian*

THE MESSIAH OF STOCKHOLM
CYNTHIA OZICK
1987

. . . the novel's simple plot lines suddenly grow thick and tangled as jungle vines and the reader starts looking around for his machete. . . . messy and world hating.

Buffalo News

Reviewer devoured by jungle vines.

THE LAST GENTLEMAN
WALKER PERCY
1966

This is a curious, unfocused novel that rambles along with the wooden, almost arthritic, gait so often found in the work of writers who begin in middle age . . . indeed, it is difficult to see what precisely the author is at . . .

New Republic

LOVE IN THE RUINS
WALKER PERCY
1971

. . . some people are going to be embarrassed by an aging liberal's earnest attempt to write a youth cult novel.

Library Journal

THE HOMECOMING
HAROLD PINTER
1965

He is more cruel, gruesome and deliberately offensive in this two-act horror than in his previous plays. On its face value, it is callous and empty enough: what lies in its Freudian depths one dreads to think.

Yorkshire Post

ZEN AND THE ART OF
MOTORCYCLE MAINTENANCE
ROBERT PIRSIG
1974

. . . a book full of grandiose promises and undelivered goods.

Commentary

THE BELL JAR
SYLVIA PLATH
1971

Highly autobiographical and . . . since it represents the views of a girl enduring a bout of mental illness, dishonest.

Atlantic Monthly

OUT OF MY LEAGUE
GEORGE PLIMPTON
1961

At first thought this seems flimsy substance for a real, live, grown-up book. It turns out that it is.

San Francisco Chronicle

A LONG AND HAPPY LIFE
REYNOLDS PRICE
1962

Very nearly a parody of the Southern Gothic novel . . . written in imitation Faulkner—a wearisome and hopeless style.

Whitney Balliett, *The New Yorker*

V.
THOMAS PYNCHON
1963

Reading *V.* is like listening to a scholarly but erratic documentation of Hell by a disinterested onlooker, while verbal sewage and vignettes of all that is most disgusting in mankind alternates with sociological asides, sardonic and blasphemous attacks on Christianity, Freudian tidbits. . . . To attempt to convey a sense of how completely boring all this melee finally is would tax the capabilities of better reviewers than myself.

Best Sellers

THE CRYING OF LOT 49
THOMAS PYNCHON
1966

. . . a curiously dead novel.

Book Week

SHAKESPEARE'S DOG
LEON ROOKE
1983

Anyone interested in conventional novels with character and plot will want to let the neighbor's mongrel chew on *Shakespeare's Dog*.

Books In Canada

Ch. Hamlet of Stratford-on-Avon, CDX

PORTNOY'S COMPLAINT
PHILIP ROTH
1969

This looks and sounds like a Jewish novel. It isn't. Or, if it is, it is not a good one, a true one . . . it is finally a definitive something or other. I regret that it is not a definitive something.

America

The best that can be said of Roth's accomplishment is that Mama Portnoy is a caricature drawn by a master cartoonist, but she's not more than that. . . . The main trouble with the Jewish family theme is that it has been overwritten.

The Nation

OUR GANG
PHILIP ROTH
1971

Nixon's rough treatment at Roth's hands may very well invite more sympathy for him than anything since the Checker's speech.

Saturday Review

THE GREAT AMERICAN NOVEL
PHILIP ROTH
1973

Roth has, most unfortunately, got into such a shouting match with his readers that some of us are going to have to start shouting back.

Encounter

MY LIFE AS A MAN
PHILIP ROTH
1974

. . . a totally solipsistic novel, which may well make it a perfect expression of the times . . .

Commentary

FRANNY AND ZOOEY
J.D. SALINGER
1961

. . . cute.

Alfred Kazin, *Atlantic Monthly*

RAISE HIGH THE ROOF BEAM CARPENTER AND SEYMOUR: AN INTRODUCTION
J.D. SALINGER
1963

. . . not even a writer of Salinger's stature—and he is our only authentic living giant—can make a god out of a suicide.

America

Hopelessly prolix . . .

New York Times Book Review

CRUCIAL CONVERSATIONS
MAY SARTON
1976

May Sarton's book reads like an unsuccessful attempt to make a Montaigne out of a molehill.

The Listener

THE HOUSE BY THE SEA
MAY SARTON
1977

I think her lack of greater popularity is due to her habit of dissecting her bowels and displaying them for public observation.

Maine Life

Maine, 1977 — the first bookectomy.

THE MAGNIFICENT SPINSTER
MAY SARTON
1986

The experience of the book, personally speaking, was like a long hike home in wet socks and gym shoes, uncomfortable and unnecessary.

Out

AMADEUS
PETER SHAFFER
1981

. . . The New York audience, the night I went, gave the play a standing ovation. A cynical friend maintains that Broadway audiences always do this to justify to themselves the mountainous cost of the evening out . . .

Robert Cushman, *Observer*

ROUGH STRIFE
LYNNE SHARON SCHWARTZ
1981

. . . almost wholly uninteresting.

Times (London)

. . . unintentionally hilarious.

Village Voice

DISTURBANCES IN THE FIELD
LYNNE SHARON SCHWARTZ
1983

. . . a fat, shapeless, talky, self-satisfied blob of a book.

Washington Post Book World

LAST EXIT TO BROOKLYN
HUBERT SELBY
1965

This is Grove Press's extra special dirty book for fall . . .

Time

THE AUTOBIOGRAPHY OF
UPTON SINCLAIR
UPTON SINCLAIR
1963

The book's value is limited, unless of course there is a socialist temperance league around somewhere.

Critic

THE BENEFACTOR
SUSAN SONTAG
1963

Mrs. Sontag is an intelligent writer who has, on her first flight, jettisoned the historical baggage of the novel. However, she has not replaced it with material or insights that carry equal or superior weight. . . . Instead she has chosen the fashionable imports of neo-existentialist philosophy and tricky contemporary techniques.

New York Times Book Review

DEATH KIT
SUSAN SONTAG
1967

. . . participates in the dull listlessness of its theme; it becomes the ennui it describes.

Christian Science Monitor

THE GIRL HUNTERS
MICKEY SPILLANE
1963

A sorry exhibit of toughness gone slimy.

New Statesman

POETS ON POETRY
WILLIAM STAFFORD
1986

. . . probably the most puzzlingly destructive and unwittingly dismissive book about poetry by a poet that has ever been written.

Ironwood

THE SPECTATOR BIRD
WALLACE STEGNER
1976

This is a dreary, contrived, mercifully short novel . . . It would seem that Stegner emptied a desk drawer and decided to make a book out of the contents. . . . This book is recommended only to the most ardent Stegner fans, and preferably those with masochistic tendencies.

Monterey Peninsula Herald

THE WINTER OF OUR DISCONTENT
JOHN STEINBECK
1961

It is regrettable that the author . . . has invested the book with a lot of mumbo-jumbo and hocus-pocus involving a talisman, a female witch and ambiguous religious significance that results in a contrived pretentious story . . .

Catholic World

This is clearly a comeback effort, and just as clearly a failure.

New Republic

SET THIS HOUSE ON FIRE
WILLIAM STYRON
1960

. . . bathetic.

Commonweal

. . . a 507 page crying jag.

Time

SCHIZOPHRENIA:
THE SACRED SYMBOL
THOMAS S. SZASZ
1976

Szasz blasts society with all the explosive force of a popgun.

Richard Jacoby, *The Nation*

THE MYTH OF MENTAL ILLNESS
THOMAS S. SZASZ
1962

The reviewer knows of no psychiatrist who agrees with Szasz and is sorry to consider his book a total waste of time.

The Psychiatric Quarterly

ON DYLAN THOMAS

A pernicious figure, one who has helped to get Wales and Welsh poetry a bad name...and done lasting harm to both.

Kingsley Amis

WHAT IS REMEMBERED
ALICE B. TOKLAS
1963

Regrettably about all Miss Toklas remembers from her famous relationship with Gertrude Stein are cool rides and cerise girdles.

Critic

THE MUSIC SCHOOL
JOHN UPDIKE
1966

As a producer of short stories, he marks time, offering only the spillover from the ever-dripping adjectival faucet...

Christian Science Monitor

RABBIT REDUX
JOHN UPDIKE
1971

Rabbit Redux is bad in all the ways *Rabbit Run* was bad, but it is bad in some different ways as well. It is a tedious album of the most futile monochromes of Sixties America: it is leering, erratic, and gimmicky; it is disingenuous and trite. At best it is dull, at worst the shabby outrage of an imagination damaged by indulgence . . .

Book World

MYRA BRECKINRIDGE
GORE VIDAL
1968

. . . a rather damp fizzle.

Library Journal

CREATION
GORE VIDAL
1981

Vidal's book is manufactured, not created.

New Statesman

BREAKFAST OF CHAMPIONS
KURT VONNEGUT
1973

From time to time it's nice to have a book you can hate—
it clears the pipes—and I hate this book.

Peter Prescott, *Newsweek*

SLAPSTICK,
OR LONESOME NO MORE
KURT VONNEGUT
1976

. . . a sorry performance, full of bored doodling.

Robert Towers, *New York Review of Books*

THE GALAPAGOS KID
LUKE WALTON
1971

. . . just terrible.

Publishers Weekly

RAT MAN OF PARIS
PAUL WEST
1986

All of this would make a great short story. Unfortunately, this is a 180 page novel.

Bestsellers

THE KANDY-KOLORED, TANGERINE-FLAKE, STREAMLINED BABY
TOM WOLFE
1965

One wants to say to Mr. Wolfe; you're so clever, you can write so well, tell us something interesting.

Saturday Review

THE PAINTED WORD
TOM WOLFE
1975

There is plenty of hot air in this particular balloon, but I don't see it going anywhere.

John Russell, *New York Times Book Review*

REVOLUTIONARY ROAD
RICHARD YATES
1961

There is a certain cheapness, even an intellectual dishonesty, in pretending that the suburbanites . . . are pseudo-vertebrates who bend in the middle when confronted by the pressures of living their own lives.

New York Herald Tribune Lively Arts

MISS MACINTOSH, MY DARLING
MARGUERITE YOUNG
1965

. . . In her zeal to demonstrate that nothing lives except in the imagination, Miss Young, with superb virtuosity, may have written a novel that in the profoundest sense does not exist.

Melvin Maddocks, *Christian Science Monitor*

FURTHER THOUGHTS ON THE ART OF REVIEWING

FURTHER THOUGHTS ON THE ART OF REVIEWING

When a man publishes a book, there are so many stupid things said that he declares he'll never do it again. The praise is almost always worse than the criticism.

SHERWOOD ANDERSON

I have long felt that any reviewer who expresses rage and loathing for a novel is preposterous. He or she is like a person who has just put on full armor and attacked a hot fudge sundae or banana split.

KURT VONNEGUT, JR.

It's surprising that authors should expect kindness to be shown to their books when they are not themselves known for kindness toward their characters, their culture or by implication their readers.

ANATOLE BROYARD

A person who publishes a book willfully appears before the populace with his pants down ... If it is a good book nothing can hurt him. If it is a bad book, nothing can help him.

EDNA ST. VINCENT MILLAY

A unanimous chorus of approval is not an assurance of survival; authors who please everyone at once are quickly exhausted.

ANDRE GIDÉ

. . . reviewers do not read books with much care . . . their profession is more given to stupidity and malice and literary ignorance even than the profession of novelist.

ANTHONY BURGESS

Some reviews give pain. This is regrettable, but no author has the right to whine. He was not obliged to be an author. He invited publicity, and he must take the publicity that comes along.

E.M. FORSTER

It is advantageous to an author that his book should be attacked as well as praised. Fame is a shuttlecock. If it be struck at one end of the room, it will soon fall to the ground. To keep it up, it must be struck at both ends.

SAMUEL JOHNSON

Nature fits all her children with something to do,
He who would write and can't write, can surely review.

JAMES RUSSELL LOWELL

FURTHER THOUGHTS ON THE ART OF REVIEWING

Confronted by an absolutely infuriating review it is sometimes helpful for the victim to do a little personal research on the critic. Is there any truth to the rumor that he had no formal education beyond the age of eleven? In any event, is he able to construct a simple English sentence? Do his participles dangle? When moved to lyricism does he write "I had a fun time"? Was he ever arrested for burglary? I don't know that you will prove anything this way, but it is perfectly harmless and quite soothing.

JEANNE KERR

Believe a woman or an epitaph,
Or any other thing that's false, before
You trust in critics.

LORD BYRON

Critics are like eunuchs in a harem. They're there every night, they see it done every night, they see how it should be done every night, but they can't do it themselves.

BRENDAN BEHAN

LETTERS

JESSICA MITFORD

I adore the first edition of *Rotten Reviews* and see therein that my collateral forebear Mary Russell Mitford slanged Jane Austen—that was a pretty silly thing for her to have done.

One problem that you may have run into when selecting from contemporary reviews is that these days reviewers are so damn polite—or I think "balanced" is the word. So that while I've had many adverse reviews over the years, they don't really qualify as rotten . . .

The best I could come up with is the enclosed from the Congressional Record . . .

William Stafford

It has sometimes occurred to me that the literary world would be much improved if critics just wrote the literature in the first place, thus avoiding that roundabout process in which the author struggles inside the complex of his book, like Laocoon contending with myriad problems, while the critic whisks through the finished book in a few minutes and immediately spots the gross blunders the author has taken a year or more to make.

ANSEL ADAMS to WALLACE STEGNER
(enclosing our reprinted review of The Spectator Bird*)*

Dear Wally,

This kind of Krap reminds me of the classic rejoinder of a musician who got a bad criticism from the London *Times*.

> Music Critic
> London Times
> London G.B.

Dear Sir:

I am sitting in a secluded small room of my apartment.

Your criticism is before me.

In a few minutes it will be behind me.

Howard Nemerov

Thanks for the invitation to RRII. The enclosed is the most recent and accessible instance; it is from Kirkus Services. I dunno what I done to these people far back in the ages, but I wish I had done it harder.

Edward Abbey

I've probably missed some good reviews of my work over the years, but never a bad one—some fellow author is always eager to tell me about the bad ones.

John Hollander

(on his review of Allen Ginsberg's Howl)

This review was written in my youth and in a sort of worked-up high dudgeon which echoed the high-camp-prophetic mode of *Howl*'s front matter, and which may have masked some of my disappointment in a turn I saw an old friend and poetic mentor to have taken. I only regret now that I hadn't given "America" and "In a Supermarket in California" time to register; I should have certainly commended them. As for not foreseeing that Allen Ginsberg would provide so much hymnody and doctrine to the counterculture which was soon to emerge, I have no regrets, having no stake in prophecy.

Rosellen Brown

Alas, though I've had some pretty dumb and even offensive things said about my work, nobody's ever managed to be particularly interesting in their dispraise. Now I'm going to crawl off and contemplate whether that's my fault or not: perhaps I don't give them enough truly interesting openings. . .?

Gay Talese

I wonder about the wisdom of resurrecting these nitwit reviews—which, being forgotten and unsuccessful in their efforts to kill off a work, are left better alone in their obscure place, no? Also, I think the worst and most mean-spirited of book critics usually get appropriate rewards for their efforts: the reviewer who was the most personally vicious about my last book is now relegated to the unenviable task of reviewing daily television.

Louis L'Amour

In the first place I do not believe writers should read reviews of their own books, and I do not. If one is not careful one is soon writing to please reviewers and not their audience or themselves. My wife occasionally reads a review to me but so far I've not had a really bad one or many would have told me . . .

I reviewed books for a time for a midwest newspaper, and afterward went into the army. One night when I was holding down the orderly room there was a telephone call asking for me. I admitted who I was, and it turned out to be an author whose book had not received a very good review from me. He said, "*Private* L'Amour, this is *Major* _____. I believe you reviewed a book of mine once."

However, he turned out to be a nice guy with no hard feelings, but for a few minutes there, he had me on my heels.

Luke Walton

You mentioned in *Rotten Reviews* that you plan a second volume of reviews and you invited submissions. Well, I enclose one from *Publishers Weekly* but I'm not famous like your other authors. I quit writing after *Publishers Weekly* told me my first novel was "just terrible." Something broke, you see. I was 29 and I'd worked for ten years at that novel, and I didn't see the point of spending another ten years only to be told the same thing again. So I tend bar here in North Plainfield, New Jersey and try to encourage the other writers who come by now and then. We don't get many writers in North Plainfield.

Luke Walton toasts his reviewer.

Isaac Asimov

Like all writers, I fume at bad reviews, and a fellow writer (Lester del Rey) once gave me some very good advice.

"When you read a review," he said, "at the very first unfavorable adjective, read no more and throw it away."

I have done that faithfully and, as a result, I have no bad reviews to send to you.

I also throw away good reviews, by the way, but I read them first.

JOYCE CAROL OATES

I have not, for obvious reasons, saved any of my multitude of "rotten reviews." This one,* though not terribly negative, just came in . . . If you think it too mild, or not outrageous, or funny, enough, maybe I could find something else. (Under a rock perhaps.) Or I could just sit back and wait for the barrage that will surely accompany my next novel.

*See *On Boxing*—ed.

Harold Brodkey

Here are some rotten reviews. I am ashamed these quotes are so stupid. I'd thought they were funnier.

Erica Jong

Since *Fear of Flying* is now a bonafide classic with ten million copies in print from Japanese to Serbo-Croat not to mention twenty other languages, this review does not have the *personal* sting it once had. Nevertheless, it broke my heart in 1974 and, in a way, is typical of the treatment fresh and radical books receive.

James Atlas

No critic who has even been through the experience of getting slammed by reviewers as I have recently can ever feel quite the same about his job. You might still be sharp in your criticism, might still render a negative verdict, but any trace of anger, sarcasm, disparagement are banished forever. You're always aware of the reality of what you're doing, of the pain, even anguish your words might cause. As I look back on some of the harsher appraisals I rendered so blithely over the years, I think: how could you have said that? Well, the job has to get done; if I don't like a book, I'm still going to say so, though in a gingerly way and with genuine remorse. As a famous but often derided novelist once said to me: they think we can take it, but we can't.

III

ROTTEN REJECTIONS

André Bernard

Editor

EDITOR'S NOTE

This book was accepted by the first publisher it was shown to. It was only later that *Rotten Rejections* itself met with rejection: one industry executive refused to discuss some now-infamous misjudgments, snarling that the very idea was "disrespectful to publishers." Another opined that both Bill Henderson and I were clearly in the terminal stages of a monstrous megalomania giving us the illusion of editorial infallibility, and who the hell were we, and hadn't we ever made a mistake! In fact, this collection contains several howlers we penned during our tenures at various publishing houses, and I assure you that Henderson and I still cringe when we see those books we so confidently, so thoroughly turned away crowding the shelves in the bookstores, inching their way into their second or fifth or tenth printings.

There have been many more rejections of books and writers later to become famous than could be included here. Some examples have simply vanished together with the houses they came from; others have been as carefully entombed as a time capsule, perhaps never to see the light of day or an inquisitive researcher's eyes again. And most rejections, alas, have been of the "not right for our list" kind, that dismal refrain editors use to accompany a graceful, painless exit. (Some of you have received your share of those letters.) We have selected instead rejections that stand on their own as minor masterpieces of the genre. Of course, everyone has wisdom in hindsight, but some of these letters were destined for greatness.

Special thanks are owed to a number of writers who dusted off old files and memories to share their experiences. Among them are Jean M. Auel, J. G. Ballard, Simon Brett, Julia Child, Mary Higgins Clark, James Dickey, Peter Dickinson, Harriet Doerr, J. P. Donleavy, Harlan Ellison, Joseph Hansen, Edward Hoagland, William Kennedy, Stephen King, James Purdy, Dr. Seuss, William L. Shirer and Julian Symons.

ANDRÉ BERNARD

INTRODUCTION

"Sorry, NO!" My first rejection slip.

It was handwritten in 1965 by Gordon "Captain Fiction" Lish, then at *Esquire,* and was in response to a story I mailed him over the transom titled "Doc Saves a Sick Whore," about a pharmacist, a whore, and a Mexican border town. I knew nothing about pharmacists, whores, or Mexican border towns. The story was awful.

Nevertheless, I found hope in that note. Gordon said he was "sorry." That probably meant he had too many manuscripts at *Esquire* and felt terrible about rejecting me. The capital "NO" and the explanation point following . . . well I chose to overlook that portion.

I wrote several more stories, all of them turned down universally, before attempting a novel. The first submission of that novel to Harper and Row's Prize Novel Contest elicited this from David Segal, editor in chief: "You have written serious fiction. The ancient and sad question is who publishes serious fiction these days." He suggested half a dozen publishers and wished me luck.

"Serious fiction!" I was overjoyed to be recognized as serious (like Melville, Faulkner, Joyce and other heroes, I figured). Again, I chose not to hear the last part of that letter, which, if I had cared to pay attention, was telling me in a nice way that my novel was unpublishable. You can't tell a 27-year old that and expect him to listen.

Years, and dozens of bland rejections later, I published the novel myself and became a publisher, one of the lower activities on the literary ladder. Now I get to send out rejections. Remembering how they sting and cripple, I try to be kind. Usually I blame Pushcart Press for being "too small" with a "limited list" for a particular manuscript. If I were young Henderson reading such a dismissal, I might infer that Pushcart was too small for my genius. Perhaps a simple NO! without the "sorry" would be more helpful for such a genius.

You will discover all sorts of rejections in André Bernard's collection of letters, in-house memos, and historical anecdotes—the first-ever such literary collection. André is a young writer with a manuscript about to make the rounds. He is also a distinguished editor now employed by one of those gigantic New York houses that eats other publishers for lunch. Plus, André has a window in his office. A sure sign of status.

André is both rejector, and soon to be rejected, perhaps. In any case, he knows what he is talking about when it comes to agony and survival.

Samuel Beckett survived: "I wouldn't touch this with a barge pole."

Harry Crews triumphed over "Burn it, son. Burn it. Fire is a great refiner."

Theodore Dreiser bested "immoral and badly written."

Tony Hillerman made it past "get rid of all that Indian stuff."

Emily Dickinson managed to ignore "Queer—the rhymes were all wrong."

And scores of other great writers did too. Evidence to follow.

I would like to honor the brave editors who admitted their mistakes and contributed letters; the publishing secretaries who clandestinely culled carbons and in-house memos from the files; and the few writers who admitted they had ever been rejected and produced the document or the memory.

On that subject, scholars beware. Some of these kiss-offs arrive from the memories of the offended and are apt to be a bit unacademic. Even the rejectors' correspondence now and then relies on memory: Pushcart's rejection of John Kennedy Toole is in my head only—and yes, I'd do it again. (Our dates are less approximate. They are the dates of rejection and/or of publication, sometimes under a different title. Some titles were never published.)

A special thanks to John White for permission to recount literary anecdotes from his *Rejection* (Addison-Wesley, 1982), an encyclopedia of all sorts of rejection; and to Jim Charlton for permission to reprint quotations from his *Writer's Quotation Book* (Pushcart, 1985), about to go into its third, revised edition, and, if I may say so, a classic. And thanks to Mary Kornblum for her beautiful design of ugly matters.

Like the previous volumes in Pushcart's Rot Series—*Rotten Reviews* and *Rotten Reviews II*—this little book is compiled for and dedicated to writers.

We hope it will leave you laughing.
And inspired to keep on writing.

BILL HENDERSON
PUBLISHER

Rejections from:

W. H. Allen Co.
American Mercury
The Atlantic
Black Mask
Bobbs, Merrill
Boni and Liveright
Jonathan Cape
Century Magazine
Chatto & Windus
Colliers
William Collins Sons
Cornhill Magazine
DAW Books
John Day
Dial
Doubleday
Duckworth
Faber & Faber
Bernard Geis
Victor Gollancz
Good Housekeeping
Good Words
Harcourt, Brace
Harper & Row
William Heinemann
Hogarth Press
Houghton Mifflin

Alfred Knopf
Little, Brown
J. B. Lippincott
Longman Group
Andrew Lytle
Macmillan
McClure's
McGraw-Hill
Methuen
Murray's Magazine
The Nation
The New Yorker
Olympia Press
The Paris Review
Prentice-Hall
Pushcart Press
Redbook
Revue de Paris
San Francisco Examiner
Saturday Evening Post
Scribner's
Secker & Warburg
The Smart Set
Vanity Fair

and others

WE THINK THE WORLD OF YOU
J. R. ACKERLEY
1960

...not nearly dirty enough and far too English.

"THE ABILITY TO KILL"
ERIC AMBLER
1963

(We) both enjoyed (this), especially that wonderful, crooked leading character—but it's all pretty rough stuff for us, so we'll have to pass...

WINESBURG, OHIO
SHERWOOD ANDERSON
1919

...far too gloomy for us.

THE CLAN OF THE CAVE BEAR
JEAN AUEL
1980

We are very impressed with the depth and scope of your research and the quality of your prose. Nevertheless, the length presents a unique problem, for production costs are rising and the reading public are reluctant to buy expensive novels unless the author has an established reputation such as the one enjoyed by James

Michener. In any case, we don't think we could distribute enough copies to satisfy you or ourselves.

NORTHANGER ABBEY
JANE AUSTEN
1818

We are willing to return the manuscript for the same (advance) as we paid for it.

Memo from George Bernard Shaw...

I finished my first book seventy-six years ago. I offered it to every publisher on the English-speaking earth I had ever heard of. Their refusals were unanimous: and it did not get into print until, fifty years later, publishers would publish anything that had my name on it. . . .

I object to publishers: the one service they have done me is to teach me to do without them. They combine commercial rascality with artistic touchiness and pettishness, without being either good business men or fine judges of literature. All that is necessary in the production of a book is an author and a bookseller, without the intermediate parasite.

BLACK OXEN
GERTRUDE ATHERTON
1923

I have no hesitation in advising you to decline Mrs. Atherton's novel . . . principally for the reason that it is an apology for adultery . . . Besides this radical immorality, the novel contains many passages of pseudo-philosophy which would give offense to religious persons.

CRASH
J. G. BALLARD
1973

The author of this book is beyond psychiatric help.

More than a dozen publishers rejected a book by the poet e e cummings. So when it was finally published it had this dedication: "No Thanks to: Farrar & Rinehart, Simon & Schuster, Coward-McCann, Limited Editions, Harcourt, Brace, Random House, Equinox Press, Smith & Haas, Viking Press, Knopf, Dutton, Harper's, Scribners, Covici, Friede." Finally published . . . by whom? By e e's mother.

> *Memo from Oliver Herford:*
>
> **M**anuscript: something submitted in haste and returned at leisure.

THE DORCHESTER TALES
JOHN BARTH
1954

Barth is really smutty, delighting in filth for its own sake, and completely incapable of being funny. What the agent hopefully calls his "great good humor" is an offensive archness and facetiousness, couched in the most stilted language and in sentences most of which are seven or so lines long.

🙞

John Barth's stories sound like a penny-whistle out of a wind-bag full of bad odors. He may have read Boccaccio and Chaucer, but he never learned their art of story-telling.

GILES GOAT-BOY
JOHN BARTH
1966

The beginning of this intrigued me; I thought, Shades of LOLITA! Paraphernalia like this means Nabokov has been more of an influence than we'd dared hope. Alas, the beginning is entirely misleading, and what emerges is a slightly ribald science fiction novel, bawdy rather than witty ... while I can see this being published, and even reviewed with puzzled respect, I don't think it will help a bit to clear up the mystery of what Barth is up to as a writer. Or possibly sell enough to pay its production costs.

DREAM OF
FAIR-TO-MIDDLING WOMEN
SAMUEL BECKETT
1932

I wouldn't touch this with a barge-pole. Beckett's probably a clever fellow, but here he has elaborated a slavish and rather incoherent imitation of Joyce, most eccentric in language and full of disgustingly affected passages—also *indecent:* the book is damned—and you wouldn't sell the book even on its title.

MOLLOY and MALONE DIES
SAMUEL BECKETT
1951

I couldn't read either book—that is, my eye refused to sit on the page and absorb meanings, or whatever substitutes for meaning in this kind of thing ... This doesn't make sense and it isn't funny ... I suspect that the real fault in these novels, if I cared to read them carefully, would be simply dullness. There's no sense considering them for publication here; the bad taste of the American public does not yet coincide with the bad taste of the French avant garde.

ZULEIKA DOBSON
MAX BEERBOHM
1911

I do not think it would interest us. The author is more highly esteemed by himself than by anyone else, and has never reached any high standard in his literary work.

THE OLD WIVES' TALE
ARNOLD BENNETT
1908

... the people themselves are so deadly and monotonously dull, so devoid of aspirations or even thoughts above the yardstick standard, so depressing and even saddening in all their social relations, that they make a most fatuous assembly to find between the covers of a book.

TALES OF SOLDIERS AND CIVILIANS
AMBROSE BIERCE
1891

... uniformly horrible and revolting. Told with some power, and now and then with strokes of wonderfully vivid description, with plots ingenious in their terror and photographic in their sickening details, we must pronounce the book too brutal to be either good art or good literature. It is the triumph of realism—realism without meaning or symbolism.

THE BRIDGE OVER THE RIVER KWAI
PIERRE BOULLE
1954

A very bad book.

THE GOOD EARTH
PEARL BUCK
1931

Regret the American public is not interested in anything on China.

Memo from Michael Joseph . . .

Publishers will tell you, with their tongue in their cheek, that every manuscript which reaches their office is faithfully read, but they are not to be believed. At least fifteen out of twenty manuscripts can be summarily rejected, usually with safety. There may be a masterpiece among them, but it is a thousand to one against.

In 1911 Marcel Proust had 800 pages of what was ultimately to become the huge complex of novels called *Remembrance of Things Past* ready for publication. Where? Who would accept such an actionless, plotless sprawl of innerness revisited? He approached the house of Fasquelle and was rejected. He went to the *Nouvelle Revue Française* and was rejected again, by a very special rejecter—the celebrated André Gide. After a third publisher, Ollendorf, had refused his manuscript (with the comment that it took him thirty pages to tell how he turned over in bed), Proust decided to pay for publication himself.

Eugène Grasset published *Du Côté de chez Swann (Swann's Way)* in November 1913. Gide read it, and the following January wrote to Proust apologizing for the rejection, which he called the "gravest error of the N.R.F. . . .one of the most burning regrets, remorses, of my life." He explained that he had considered Proust a "snob" and a "social butterfly," had only glanced at his manuscript, and had been unimpressed by what he had glimpsed. He asked pardon. Proust forgave him and the two became good friends.

THE OUTLAW OF TORN
EDGAR RICE BURROUGHS
1927

I am not sure there is any particular value in the happy ending. It seems to be more legitimate to have both De Vac and the outlaw die in the end, leaving the lady dissolved in tears, possibly on her way to become a nun . . .

Irving Stone's first book was about Van Gogh. He took it to Alfred Knopf, and "they never opened it—the package with the manuscript got home before I did." After fifteen more rejections the book, *Lust for Life,* was finally accepted and published in 1934. It has now sold about twenty-five million copies.

UNDER THE MOONS OF MARS
EDGAR RICE BURROUGHS
1912

It is not at all probable, we think, that we can make use of the story of a Virginia soldier of fortune miraculously transported to Mars . . .

OLD CREOLE DAYS
GEORGE WASHINGTON CABLE
1879

Although we can assure you that we fully appreciate your Stories both for their originality and merit we must... after due consideration decline their publication... the *times* are not particularly promising and collections of short stories almost always unsaleable. Your proposition to furnish a list of 500 subscribers is of course an inducement but not a sufficient one.

THE POSTMAN ALWAYS RINGS TWICE
JAMES M. CAIN
1934

...I think it is only a matter of time before you reach out into more substantial efforts that will be capable of making some real money as books.

MASTERING THE ART OF FRENCH COOKING
JULIA CHILD, SIMONE BECK, LOUISETTE BERTHOLLE
1961

What we envisage as saleable... is perhaps a series of small books devoted to particular portions of the meal... We also feel that such a series should meet a rigorous standard of simplicity and compactness, certainly less elaborate than your present volumes, which, although we are sure are foolproof, are undeniably demanding in the time and focus of the cook, who is so apt to be mother, nurse, chauffeur, and cleaner as well.

&

... It is a big, expensive cookbook of elaborate information and might well prove formidable to the American housewife. She might easily clip one of these recipes out of a magazine but be frightened by the book as a whole.

Memo from Stephen King:

Early in the 1970s, before my first novel (*Carrie*) was published, I sent three chapters and an outline of a science fiction novel I'd written to a publisher. Three weeks after submission, I received my material back in the SASE with a note which was both cordial and frosty. "We are not interested in science fiction which deals with negative utopias," the letter said. "They do not sell." I muttered a few words to my wife—something to the effect that George Orwell and Jonathan Swift had done quite well with negative utopias—and tossed the book in a drawer, where it stayed for eight or nine years.

THE MYSTERIOUS AFFAIR AT STYLES
AGATHA CHRISTIE
1920

It is very interesting and has several good points, but it is not quite suitable for our list.

"JOURNEY BACK TO LOVE"
MARY HIGGINS CLARK
1962

We found the heroine as boring as her husband had.

CLAUDINE IN SCHOOL
COLETTE
1900

I wouldn't be able to sell 10 copies.

THE FLYING SWANS
PADRAIC COLUM
1957

... you get almost no sensation of a story being told, for the mind of the author and that very difficult Irish way of speaking English both get in the way.

FREYE OF THE SEVEN ISLES
JOSEPH CONRAD
1911

Its overpowering gloom makes it impossible for serialization.

WHITE BUILDINGS
HART CRANE
1926

...one has to live in a mundane world... So I am afraid that we will have to pass up *White Buildings*... It is really the most perplexing kind of poetry. One reads it with a growing irritation, not at you but at himself, for the denseness of one's own intellect.

Sometimes it seems—to writers—that the number of possible rejections of a would-be book is limited only by the number of publishers. Says the *Guinness Book of World Records*, "The greatest number of publishers' rejections for a manuscript is 106 for *World Government Crusade* by Gilbert Young..."

MAGGIE: A GIRL OF THE STREETS
STEPHEN CRANE
1893

. . . too cruel for us.

UNPUBLISHED STORY COLLECTION
HARRY CREWS
1956

Burn it, son, burn it. Fire is a great refiner.

THE IPCRESS FILE
LEN DEIGHTON
1963

Not only does this bog down in the middle, but the author tends to stay too long with non-essentials. He seems to have little idea of pace, and is enchanted with his words, his tough style, and that puts me off badly . . .

YOUNG RENNY
MAZO DE LA ROCHE
1935

Mary is wooden, Malahide a caricature, (this) is a failure and will, if published, end the Whiteoak family once and for all. It will have a disastrous effect upon your public.

"SORROWS OF CHILDHOOD"
CHARLES DICKENS
1852

I am sorry, but Brutus sacrifices unborn children of his own as well as those of other people—the "Sorrows of Childhood," long in type and long a mere mysterious name, must come out. The paper really is, like the celebrated ambassadorial appointment, "too bad."

Dickens cutting his own work from Household Words

INTO THE STONE, AND OTHER POEMS
JAMES DICKEY
1959

There's a fascination about these ... yet I simply haven't the faintest idea what he's talking about most of the time. I like cryptograms very much, but you can't send a code book along with a book of poems, and I soon get impatient not knowing the answers. We're in the communications business, aren't we?

Memo from Patrick Dennis ...

Auntie Mame circulated for five years, through the halls of fifteen publishers, and finally ended up with Vanguard Press, which, as you can see, is rather deep into the alphabet.

EARLY, UNTITLED POETRY MANUSCRIPT
EMILY DICKINSON
1862

Queer—the rhymes were all wrong.

❧

They are quite as remarkable for defects as for beauties and are generally devoid of true poetical qualities.

Before William Saroyan (who became one of this country's most published authors) got his first acceptance he had a pile of rejection slips thirty inches high—maybe seven thousand in all.

William Saroyan rejected the 1940 Pulitzer Prize for his play *The Time of Your Life* because, he said, business had no business judging art.

WELCOME TO HARD TIMES
E. L. DOCTOROW
1960

Things improve a bit with the rebuilding of the village but then go to hell in a hack at the end. Perhaps there is a public that can take all this with a straight face but I'm not one of them.

STONES FOR IBARRA
HARRIET DOERR
1984

As it now stands, the only thing resembling a plot in this book is the slow deterioration of the husband's health... Perhaps if the book were reconceived as order, rationalism, industry and health struggling against chaos, fate, inertia and disease, it might pull together into an integral novel of universal scope.

THE GINGER MAN
J. P. DONLEAVY
1955

... publication of *The Ginger Man* would not be a practical proposition in this country. So much of the text would have to be excised that it would almost destroy the story, and even a certain amount of rewriting would not overcome the problem... I do not think you will find another publisher who would be willing to undertake the publication under present circumstances.

Dr. Laurence J. Peter's competence as a discover of principles was not initially recognized. When he first submitted the manuscript of *The Peter Principle: Why Things Always Go Wrong* to McGraw-Hill in 1964, the editor replied: "I can foresee no commercial possibilities for such a book and consequently can offer no encouragement."

Thirty publishers and thirty turndowns later, William Morrow & Co. paid $2,500 for the manuscript and ordered a printing of 10,000 copies. No one expected the book to be a big hit but it sold more than 200,000 copies in its first year, was on the *New York Times* best-seller list through 1970 and was translated into thirty-eight languages.

THE GREAT DAYS
JOHN DOS PASSOS
1958

I am rather offended by what seems to me quite gratu-
itous passages dealing with sex acts and natural func-
tions.

A STUDY IN SCARLET
ARTHUR CONAN DOYLE
1887

Neither long enough for a serial nor short enough for a
single story.

SISTER CARRIE
THEODORE DREISER
1900

... I cannot conceive of the book arousing the interest
or inviting the attention ... of the feminine readers
who control the destinies of so many novels.

❧

... immoral and badly written ... the choice of your
characters has been unfortunate ... not the best kind of
book for a young author to make his first book.

THE TITAN
THEODORE DREISER
1914

If it is too strong for Harper then it would surely be too rich for us.

ISABEL OF BAVARIA
ALEXANDRE DUMAS
1834

Stick to drama, my dear fellow. You know you are dramatic through and through.

THE SILENCE OF HISTORY
JAMES T. FARRELL
1963

Although these manuscripts are physically a mess, they are also lousy.

SANCTUARY
WILLIAM FAULKNER
1931

Good God, I can't publish this. We'd both be in jail.

As might be expected, James Joyce's writings excited some splendidly grandiose rejections. His *Dubliners* was refused by twenty-two publishers and then shot down in flames by an irate citizen. As Joyce reported it, "When at last it was printed some very kind person bought out the entire edition and had it burnt in Dublin—a new and private *auto-da-fé*." The odyssey of his *Ulysses* was even more spectacular—it was rejected, in fire, by two governments. Parts of the novel were serialized in the New York *Little Review* in 1918–20, and after rejection by a U.S. publisher the whole book was published in France in 1922 by Sylvia Beach's Shakespeare Press. Copies were sent to America and England. They were, reported Joyce, "Seized and burnt by the Custom authorities of New York and Folkestone." Not until 1933 was the U.S. ban on *Ulysses* lifted; the book was published by Random House the following year.

SARTORIS
WILLIAM FAULKNER
1929

If the book had a plot and structure, we might suggest shortening and revisions but it is so diffuse that I don't think this would be any use. My chief objection is that you don't have any story to tell.

THIS SIDE OF PARADISE
F. SCOTT FITZGERALD
1920

... the story does not seem to work up to a conclusion;—neither the hero's career nor his character are shown to be brought to any stage which justifies an ending ... It seems to us in short that the story does not culminate in anything ...

"THUMBS UP"
F. SCOTT FITZGERALD
1936

I thought it was swell but all the femmes down here said it was horrid. The thumbs, I suppose, were too much for them.

"THOUSAND AND FIRST SHIP"
F. SCOTT FITZGERALD
1936

We have pondered for a long while over this Scott Fitzgerald poem only to conclude reluctantly that we should not take it. As a poem, it has certain grave defects, including the non-permissible rhyme in the fourth stanza ...

MADAME BOVARY
GUSTAVE FLAUBERT
1856

You have buried your novel underneath a heap of details which are well done but utterly superfluous . . .

THE DIARY OF ANNE FRANK
ANNE FRANK
1952

The girl doesn't, it seems to me, have a special perception or feeling which would lift that book above the "curiosity" level.

Memo from John Gardner . . .

One should fight like the devil the temptation to think well of editors. They are all, without exception—at least some of the time—incompetent or crazy. By the nature of their profession they read too much, with the result they grow jaded and cannot recognize talent though it dances in front of their eyes.

---

*P**eyton Place,* that ersatz *Desire Under the Elms,* a mish-mash of small-town sex steamy enough to tempt, you would think, all profit-minded publishers (and what other kind, you might ask, is there?), was turned down by fourteen of them. A work as different from *Peyton Place* as can be imagined, William Appleman Williams's *The Tragedy of American Diplomacy,* was rejected by more than twenty publishers before it was finally accepted. It has now been reprinted several times and is recognized as an outstanding revisionist work. *Jonathan Livingston Seagull* also flew through some twenty rejections.

"THE LONELY"
PAUL GALLICO
1937

My dear boy, what a masterpiece! How beautifully thought out! What color, what fire! It's truly magnificent writing. It's so poetic. Do take it over to *Harper's Bazaar* where they will really know how to appreciate it.

A MAN OF PROPERTY
(from THE FORSYTE SAGA)
JOHN GALSWORTHY
1906

Take your long novel down the street to my friend William Heinemann who specializes in fiction, and sit down and write a play for me—I think you'd do *that* well.

❧

This author writes to please himself rather than to please the novel reading public and accordingly his novel lacks popular qualities ... the average reader may be pardoned if he fails to become interested in the intricate family relations involved in the opening chapters of the book ... from beginning to end there is not one really admirable character, and it is hard to feel sympathy even for those who undergo sorrow and suffering.

❧

... the slight plot, the fact that all the characters are distinctly British, both seem to make it clear that the volume would not have any real sale in this country ...

"THE SHRIEKING SKELETON"
ERLE STANLEY GARDNER
1937

The characters talk like dictionaries, the so-called plot has whiskers on it like Spanish moss hanging from a live oak in a Louisiana bayou.

"MRS GRUNDY'S ENEMIES"
GEORGE GISSING
1882

It is too painful and would not attract the kind of reader who subscribes to our publications.

THE DESCENDANT
ELLEN GLASGOW
1897

Morbid, untrue to life and untrue to American social conditions. It looks as if the author had studied New York from a winter spent at a New York hotel.

James M. Cain's novel *The Postman Always Rings Twice* stirred up something of a sensation when it was first published in 1934. It wasn't about the postal service, it was about sex. Cain explained that he had given his book its odd title because before it was accepted for publication it was rejected many times, and each day that the postman brought a letter of rejection he rang twice.

THREE WEEKS
ELINOR GLYN
1897

This is pure bosh . . . impossible sentimental gush from first to last.

THE VISITS OF ELIZABETH
ELINOR GLYN
1907

All the men, married and single, make love to her in various ways, and she comments naively on their behavior in squeezing her arms, holding her hands, kissing her, etc. . . . At the end one has the uncomfortable feeling of having been a spectator of the operation of rubbing the bloom off a girl by a lot of worldly and more or less vulgar people.

LORD OF THE FLIES
WILLIAM GOLDING
1954

It does not seem to us that you have been wholly successful in working out an admittedly promising idea.

THE WIND IN THE WILLOWS
KENNETH GRAHAME
1908

. . . the form of the story is most unexpected.

THE TIN DRUM
GÜNTER GRASS
1961

It can never be translated.

THE WHITE GODDESS
ROBERT GRAVES
1948

I have to say that it was beyond me and failed to stir any spark of interest... A publisher frequently publishes many books which are too good for him, i.e. they transcend his individual taste and scholarship, but at least he has some inkling of what the author is aiming at and can see that there is some reasonable ground for publication. Here it seems to me that the interest is so obscure and so limited... You need for this book a publisher who is humble enough to take it *ex cathedra.*

GREEK GODS AND HEROES
ROBERT GRAVES
1960

... Graves has climbed on his hobby horse and ridden off on it. The hobby horse is anger at the Freudian and Jungian interpretation of the myths... (this) will arouse controversy instead of assent.

Memo from a Chinese Economic Journal...

We have read your manuscript with boundless delight. If we were to publish your paper, it would be impossible for us to publish any work of lower standard. And as it is unthinkable that in the next thousand years we shall see its equal, we are, to our regret, compelled to return your divine composition, and to beg you a thousand times to overlook our short sight and timidity.

THE LAST OF THE PLAINSMEN
ZANE GREY
1908

I do not see anything in this to convince me you can write either narrative or fiction.

RIDERS OF THE PURPLE SAGE
ZANE GREY
1912

It is offensive to broadminded people who do not believe that it is wise to criticize any one denomination or religious belief.

Lee Pennington has been published in more than 300 magazines—and rejected so many thousand times that in one six-month period he papered all four walls of a room with rejection slips. ("I loved getting the $8\frac{1}{2} \times 11$ rejections more than the 3×5 ones because they covered more space.") He has also filled scrapbooks with rejection slips, used them for coasters, and given rejection parties—invitations written on the backs of rejection slips.

Other suggested uses for those slips: make lampshades of them, laminate coffee tables with them, make (as did Muriel Rukeyser) wastebaskets of them. Put them on the refrigerator so you won't eat so much.

Pennington once wrote a poem about William Faulkner, sent it off, and got back a two-page single-spaced rejection, the first two sentences of which read, "This is the worst poem in the English language. You are the worst poet in the English language." He burned that rejection letter (an act he has since repented—it would have graced his scrapbook) and sent the poem to another magazine, which accepted it "with glowing praise," and chose it as its year's best poem.

"POEM"
SARA HAARDT
1923

The poem I can't take. We have 200 or 300 bales of poetry stored in Hoboken, in the old Norddeutscher-Lloyd pier. There are 300,000 poets in America.

THE WELL OF LONELINESS
RADCLYFFE HALL
1928

... we do feel (and this is the fundamental reason for our decision not to publish) that the book will be regarded as propaganda, and that inevitably the publishers of it will have to meet not only severe criticism but a chorus of fanatical abuse which, although unjustifiable, may nevertheless do them considerable damage. That consequence we are not prepared to face, and so we must decline the book...

THE MAN EVERYBODY WAS AFRAID OF
JOSEPH HANSEN
1975

This was put together with chewing gum and paper clips.

DESPERATE REMEDIES
THOMAS HARDY
1871

... the story is ruined by the disgusting and absurd outrage which is the key to its mystery. The violation of a young lady at an evening party, and the subsequent birth of a child, is too abominable to be tolerated ...

TESS OF THE D'URBERVILLES
THOMAS HARDY
1891

... improper explicitness.

THE POOR MAN AND THE LADY
THOMAS HARDY
1868

... there crops up in parts a certain rawness of absurdity that is very displeasing, and makes it read like some clever lad's dream: the thing hangs too loosely together ... half worthy of Balzac.

CATCH-22
JOSEPH HELLER
1961

I haven't really the foggiest idea about what the man is trying to say. It is about a group of American Army officers stationed in Italy, sleeping (but not interestingly) with each others' wives and Italian prostitutes, and talking unintelligibly to one another. Apparently the author intends it to be funny—possibly even satire—but it is really not funny on any intellectual level. He has two devices, both bad, which he works constantly . . . This, as you may imagine, constitutes a continual and unmitigated bore.

&

It is always possible that a reader who goes in for this zany-epigram stuff will think it is a work of genius, and of course he may be right. But from your long publishing experience you will know that it is less disastrous to turn down a work of genius than to turn down talented mediocrities.

THE TORRENTS OF SPRING
ERNEST HEMINGWAY
1926

It would be in extremely rotten taste, to say nothing of being horribly cruel, should we want to publish it.

There was once in Paris a society composed of playwrights who had been hissed. They met once a month on an ill-omened day, Friday, and among their members were the young Dumas, Zola, and Offenbach.

Rudyard Kipling was rejected three times for his country's highest literary honor. He was a world famous writer when Tennyson's death left the post of Great Britain's Poet Laureate vacant in 1892. Kipling was passed over and the honor was given to a relatively unknown author, Alfred Austin. When Austin died in 1913 Kipling was even more famous—in 1907 he had won the Nobel Prize for literature; again he was rejected for a less eminent writer, Robert Bridges. In 1930 the title was given to John Masefield.

It has been said that one reason for Kipling's rejections was his poem "The Widow at Windsor," which cast Victoria as a Queen whose dominions cost the lives of her soldiers.

KON-TIKI
THOR HEYERDAHL
1952

The idea of men adrift on a raft does have a certain appeal, but for the most part this is a long, solemn and tedious Pacific voyage.

THE BLESSING WAY
TONY HILLERMAN
1970

If you insist on rewriting this, get rid of all that Indian stuff.

Memo from Edward Hoagland...

There's no percentage in a publisher writing nasty letters to authors, even those whom he is rejecting; instead, the practice is likely to rebound to his disadvantage later on. Most editors, in fact, train themselves to write blandly agreeable or at least tactful letters to all the writers they must correspond with. It becomes a professional handicap for them if they do not learn this form of discipline as a part of their trade. Writers are grudge-holders, and in their solitude will nurse and magnify any grievance and pass on news of it to other writers for the next decade. Reviewers are much more likely to go haywire with spleen... I was once rejected for an advanced writing course at Harvard because X thought that reading my first novel, *Cat Man,* felt like "being thrown into a bucket of blood," though he added that I "might be published with acclaim some day."

"THE PENSION GRILLPARZER"
(from THE WORLD ACCORDING TO GARP)
JOHN IRVING
1979

... only mildly interesting... it contributes nothing new to either language or form.

THE SKETCH BOOK
WASHINGTON IRVING
1819

I entreat you to believe that I feel truly obligated by your most kind intentions towards me, and that I entertain the most unfeigned respect for your most tasteful talents. My house is completely filled with workpeople at this time, and I have only an office to transact business in; and yesterday I was wholly occupied, or I should have done myself the pleasure of seeing you. If it would not suit me to engage in the publication of your present work, it is only because I do not see that scope in the nature of it which would enable me to make those satisfactory accounts between us, without which I really feel no satisfaction in engaging.

IN THE CAGE
HENRY JAMES
1898

A duller story I have never read. It wanders through a deep mire of affected writing and gets nowhere, tells no tale, stirs no emotion but weariness. The professional critics who mistake an indirect and roundabout use of words for literary art will call it an excellent piece of work; but people who have any blood in their veins will yawn and throw it down—if, indeed, they ever pick it up.

"THE SACRED FOUNT"
HENRY JAMES
1901

It is surely the n + 1st power of Jamesiness . . . It gets decidedly on one's nerves. It is like trying to make out page after page of illegible writing. The sense of effort becomes acutely exasperating. Your spine curls up, your hair-roots prickle & you want to get up and walk around the block. There is no story—oh! but none at all . . . the *subject* is something to guess, guess all the time.

POEMS
ORRICK JOHNS
1916

I have read these poems seventy or eighty times but they still fail to give me anything even remotely approaching a thrill. My private conviction is that they are very bad, but in this I may be wrong. Why not mock me and put me to fright by sending in some superb and undoubted masterpiece?

Lewis Carroll rejected rather than was rejected, pictures rather than words. He paid for initial publication of *Alice's Adventures in Wonderland* (then titled *Alice's Adventures Under Ground*) by Macmillan in 1865 but he and his illustrator, John Tenniel, were dissatisfied with the quality of the reproductions in the first printing and rejected it. (Subsequent printings pleased author, illustrator, publisher and public.) Carroll got another artist, Henry Holiday, to illustrate *The Hunting of the Snark,* published by Macmillan in 1876, but he rejected one of Holiday's pictures, a very important one. It will be remembered that the *Hunting* ends when the Baker meets the Snark, shrieks, and disappears—because the Snark is a Boojum and as everybody knows it is

POMES PENYEACH
JAMES JOYCE
1927

They belong in the bible or the family album with the portraits.

the fate of whoever meets a Boojum to "softly and suddenly vanish away." Holiday drew a picture of the Boojum as a great squat indistinct figure radiating mindless power, and very frightening indeed. Carroll rejected it because it was too good. The unimaginable had been imagined, and that shouldn't be.

In 1889 Macmillan published a juvenile version of *Alice* (which psychologists never tire of saying is not really a children's book) with twenty of the Tenniel pictures enlarged and colored, and Carroll rejected the first printing because, he said, the colors were too gaudy. The rejected books were sent to a New York publisher who re-rejected them because, he said, the colors were too dull.

A PORTRAIT OF THE ARTIST AS A YOUNG MAN
JAMES JOYCE
1916

. . . rather discursive and the point of view is not an attractive one.

❧

It is not possible to get hold of an intelligent audience in wartime.

≈

... a good bit of work but it won't pay.

≈

There are many *longueurs*. Passages which, though the publisher's reader may find them interesting, will be tedious to the ordinary man among the reading public. That public will call the book, as it stands at present, realistic, unprepossessing, unattractive... It is too discursive, formless, unrestrained, and ugly things, ugly words, are too prominent; indeed at times they seem to be shoved in one's face, on purpose, unnecessarily. The point of view will be voted "a little sordid." ... And at the end of the book there is a complete falling to bits; the pieces of writing and the thoughts are all in pieces and they fall like damp, ineffective rockets.

ULYSSES
JAMES JOYCE
1922

We have read the chapters of Mr. Joyce's novel with great interest, and we wish we could offer to print it. But the length is an insuperable difficulty to us at present. We can get no one to help us, and at our rate of progress a book of 300 pages would take at least two years to produce ... I have told my servants to send the MS back to you.

THE ODYSSEY: A MODERN SEQUEL
NIKOS KAZANTZAKIS
1959

... this is a very confused affair, muddling up allusions from various mythologies, religions and literatures ... I found the whole performance a bore.

Emily Dickinson had only seven of her poems published in her lifetime (now her collected words actually fill a fat volume) but her rejecter became her friend. In 1858 Thomas Wentworth Higginson of the *Atlantic Monthly* issued an appeal for fresh talent and the Belle of Amherst sent him some of her poems. He thought her a "half-cracked poetess" and advised her not to try to get anything published. But he did offer friendship and they corresponded for several years.

IRONWEED
WILLIAM KENNEDY
1983

There is much about the novel that is very good and much that I did not like. When I throw in the balance the book's unrelenting lack of commerciality, I am afraid I just have to pass.

❧

I like William Kennedy but not enough. He's a very good writer, something no one needs to tell you or him, and his characters are terrific. I cannot explain turning this down.

SEVEN STREAMS OF NEVIS
GALWAY KINNELL
1958

I doubt that it would arouse Lamont enthusiasm—more probably it would be a cause of Lamontation.

UNTITLED SUBMISSION
RUDYARD KIPLING
1889

I'm sorry, Mr. Kipling, but you just don't know how to use the English language.

A SEPARATE PEACE
JOHN KNOWLES
1958

... embarrassingly overwrought ... strikes me as much overdone, and even pretentious ... I feel rather hopeless about his having a future.

JERUSALEM
SELMA LAGERLOF
1901

An inordinately long love story, well up toward 200,000 words ... has some unwelcome episodes of illegitimacy.

LADY CHATTERLEY'S LOVER
D. H. LAWRENCE
1928

For your own good do not publish this book.

THE RAINBOW
D. H. LAWRENCE
1915

It is unpublishable as it stands because of its flagrant love passages.

What ultimately became one of the favorite children's books of all time *The Tale of Peter Rabbit,* was prenatally "courteously rejected" by the English publisher Frederick Warne and then "returned with or without thanks by at least six [other] firms," author-illustrator Beatrix Potter noted. (According to an almost certainly apocryphal story one rejecter commented that the tale "smelled like rotting carrots.") Finally she took her savings and paid for publication herself. The little book sold so well that Warne changed his mind, took over publication, and voilà! That was more than eighty years ago, and Peter Rabbit and his friends are still selling briskly.

THE SPY WHO CAME IN FROM THE COLD
JOHN LE CARRÉ
1963

You're welcome to le Carré—he hasn't got any future.

RHYMES TO BE TRADED FOR BREAD
VACHEL LINDSAY
1912

Unpoetical poems, privately printed in pretentious but poor style.

"THE LAW OF LIFE"
JACK LONDON
1900

. . . forbidding and depressing.

GENTLEMEN PREFER BLONDES
ANITA LOOS
1925

Do you realize, young woman, that you're the first American writer ever to poke fun at sex?

Memo from Julian Symons . . .

My own first book, *The Immaterial Murder Case*, was turned down in the U.S. They wrote me a first paragraph about it that was full of praise, saying it was wonderfully funny, enjoyed reading it enormously, etc. Then the second part said: afraid it's not right for us, can't publish it, shall we destroy the ms or would you like it back!

There is a story in the trade that a publisher once accepted a book and sent it to an artist for illustrations. When he had finished, the artist sent the manuscript back—and it was returned to him with a rejection slip.

MAN MEETS DOG
KONRAD LORENZ
1952

... not quite important enough to translate and set up in competition with the many dog books that bark for attention.

UNDER THE VOLCANO
MALCOLM LOWRY
1947

Flashbacks on the character's past lives and past and present thoughts and emotions (are) often tedious and unconvincing... The book is *much too long* and over elaborate for its content... The author has overreached himself and is given to eccentric word-spinning and too much stream-of-consciousness stuff.

❧

Its quality is too rare to be successful.

A RIVER RUNS THROUGH IT
NORMAN MACLEAN
1976

These stories have trees in them.

THE DEER PARK
NORMAN MAILER
1955

This will set publishing back 25 years.

THE NAKED AND THE DEAD
NORMAN MAILER
1948

All other considerations which this book presents are subsidiary to the problem posed by the profanity and obscenity of its dialogue. In my opinion it is barely publishable.

THE ASSISTANT
BERNARD MALAMUD
1957

... superficial and unconvincing ... I do not see this book as a very well told story on any level. I do not think it would have either a good critical reception or substantial sales. Cumulatively depressing.

THE LATE GEORGE APLEY
JOHN P. MARQUAND
1936

Unpublishable.

In 1969 *Steps,* a novel by Jerzy Kosinski, won the National Book Award. Six years later a freelance writer named Chuck Ross, to test the old theory that a novel by an unknown writer doesn't have a chance, typed the first twenty-one pages of *Steps* and sent them out to four publishers as the work of "Erik Demos." All four rejected the manuscript. Two years after that he typed out the whole book and sent it, again credited to Erik Demos, to more publishers, including the original publisher of the Kosinski book, Random House. Again, all rejected it with unhelpful comments—Random House used a form letter. Altogether, fourteen publishers (and thirteen literary agents) failed to recognize a book that had already been published and had won an important prize.

"A FLEA STORY"
DON MARQUIS
1927

We like it but it is over the heads of our readers.

BRUTAL AND LICENTIOUS
JOHN MASTERS
1958

Retired curry colonels writing their reminiscences of India are two a penny.

THE RAZOR'S EDGE
W. SOMERSET MAUGHAM
1944

Not desirable. I do not find the thing good of its kind and few people like that kind... Some of the talk is clever and some of the characters interesting, but much of the long discussion of the author's philosophy of life is tedious and the author's view pessimistic and hopeless... I do not think that the book would have a large sale here, and while I would not say that it is impossible, I think it is distasteful.

MOBY-DICK
HERMAN MELVILLE
1851

We regret to say that our united opinion is entirely against the book as we do not think it would be at all suitable for the Juvenile Market in [England.] It is very long, rather old-fashioned, and in our opinion not deserving of the reputation which it seems to enjoy.

TYPEE
HERMAN MELVILLE
1846

It is impossible that it could be true and therefore it is without real value.

PEYTON PLACE
GRACE METALIOUS
1955

Definitely too racy for us.

ESTHER WATERS
GEORGE MOORE
1894

We like the story ourselves but there are scenes in it such as a childbirth in a hospital with full accounts of labor pains etc., which would hardly go down here and it would certainly excite surprise if published by us.

WHEN Kathleen Windsor's bawdy novel, *Forever Amber*, was banned in Boston (and the rest of Massachusetts) a full two years after it was published, the state's attorney general, George Rowell, contended that the book was obscene and that bookstores carrying it were liable for criminal action. The well-minded prosecutor came up with the following analysis of the book:

- 70 references to sexual intercourse
- 39 references to illegitimate pregnancies
- 7 abortions
- 10 descriptions of women dressing or undressing in the presence of men
- 5 references to incest and 10 to the badger game
- 13 {references} ridiculing marriage
- 49 "miscellaneous objectional passages"

Rowell ended his rejection of the novel by stating, "The references to women's bosoms and other parts of their anatomy were so numerous I did not even attempt to count them." The banning was eventually repealed but did help propel the sales of *Forever Amber* upward two million copies.

E dward Fitzgerald sent the manuscript of his *The Rubáiyát of Omar Khayyám* to the editor of Fraser's Magazine in 1858.

He waited one year for a reply.

But he heard nothing.

He retrieved the manuscript and published it himself—to great success.

AFFAIRS OF THE HEART
MALCOLM MUGGERIDGE
1950

... the author's writing deteriorates in a peculiarly striking fashion as he lays about him with his satirical club ... a very mystifying and unsatisfactory product for the American market.

LOLITA
VLADIMIR NABOKOV
1955

It should be, and probably has been, told to a psycho-analyst, and it has been elaborated into a novel which contains some wonderful writing, but it is overwhelmingly nauseating, even to an enlightened Freudian. To

the public, it will be revolting. It will not sell, and it
will do immeasurable harm to a growing reputation . . .
It is a totally perverse performance all around . . . the
whole thing is an unsure cross between hideous reality
and improbable fantasy. It often becomes a wild neu-
rotic daydream, and the plot often gets confused, especially in the chase parts . . . It comes out as ghastly self-
savagery. I am most disturbed at the thought that the
writer has asked that this be published. I can see no
possible cause could be served by its publication now. I
recommend that it be buried under a stone for a thousand years.

PNIN
VLADIMIR NABOKOV
1957

. . . if we published it as a novel we should be blamed
by the reviewers for presenting it under false pretences.
And if we publish it as a collection of stories, we'd have
trouble getting it read . . .

THE IMAGE AND THE LAW
HOWARD NEMEROV
1947

If the object of poetry is obscurity, Howard Nemerov is
a great poet . . . I am, perhaps, a confirmed reactionary
in poetry, preferring "I stood upon a little hill" and . . .

"Pepsicola hits the spot for just a nickel you get a lot" . . . Nuts, I say.

THE FOUR-CHAMBERED HEART
ANAÏS NIN
1950

Miss Nin's usual rather sensitive and lyrical writing on her usual theme of erotica interlarded with psychoanalytic interpretations . . . Miss Nin is distinctly caviar to the general public but I'm afraid it's only red caviar at that . . .

ANIMAL FARM
GEORGE ORWELL
1945

I am highly critical of many aspects of internal and external Soviet policy; but I could not possibly publish . . . a general attack of this kind.

&.

It is impossible to sell animal stories in the U.S.A.

&.

. . . highly ill-advised to publish at the present time . . . Another thing: it would be less offensive if the predominant caste in the fable were not pigs. I think the choice of pigs as the ruling caste will no doubt give offense to many people, and particularly to anyone who is a bit touchy, as undoubtedly the Russians are . . .

ớ

... your pigs are far more intelligent than the other an-
imals, and therefore the best qualified to run the
farm—in fact, there couldn't have been an Animal
Farm at all without them: so what was needed was not
more communism but more public-spirited pigs.

DOWN AND OUT IN PARIS AND LONDON
GEORGE ORWELL
1933

It is decidedly too short...

THE SEA GOD
GEORGE ORWELL
1929

... immature and unsatisfactory... I think, too, that
you deal with sex too much in your writings. Subjects a
little less worldly would have a greater appeal!

THE LABYRINTH OF SOLITUDE
OCTAVIO PAZ
1962

I don't see that the whole book could be of interest
to American readers. This is because it is *addressed* to
Mexicans...

FOLIO CLUB TALES
EDGAR ALLAN POE
1836

Readers in this country have a decided and strong preference for works... in which a single and connected story occupies the entire volume.

A southern writer named John Kennedy Toole wrote a comic novel about life in New Orleans called *A Confederacy of Dunces*. It was so relentlessly rejected by publishers that he killed himself. That was in 1969. His mother refused to give up on the book. She sent it out and got it back, rejected, over and over again. At last she won the patronage of Walker Percy, who got it accepted by the Louisiana State University Press, and in 1980 it won the Pulitzer Prize for fiction.

Memo from Samuel Johnson . . .

Your manuscript is both good and original; but the part that is good is not original, and the part that is original is not good.

THE CHOSEN
CHAIM POTOK
1967

. . . too long, too static, too repetitious, too ponderous and a long list of other negative "toos" . . . he has no novelistic sense whatever; he just tells you every blessed thing that the characters said and did and thought in the order in which it occurred . . . most of the time it is solidly, monumentally boring.

"PORTRAIT D'UNE FEMME"
EZRA POUND
1912

The opening line contains too many "r"s.

A DANCE TO THE MUSIC OF TIME
ANTHONY POWELL
1960

... almost too obviously Proustian in its gossipy, inconsequential detail ... a 350,000 word monstrosity that may not be any more saleable than its parts have proved.

SWANN'S WAY (REMEMBRANCE OF THINGS PAST)
MARCEL PROUST
1913

My dear fellow, I may be dead from the neck up, but rack my brains as I may I can't see why a chap should need thirty pages to describe how he turns over in bed before going to sleep.

❧

I only troubled myself so far as to open one of the notebooks of your manuscripts; I opened it at random, and, as ill luck would have it, my attention soon plunged into the cup of camomile tea on page 62—then tripped, at page 64, on the phrase ... where you speak of the "visible vertebra of a forehead."

MALCOLM
JAMES PURDY
1960

Incomprehensible.

AN UNSUITABLE ATTACHMENT
BARBARA PYM
1963

Novels like (this), despite their qualities, are getting increasingly difficult to sell.

THE SWEET DOVE DIED
BARBARA PYM
1978

Not the kind of thing to which people are turning.

In 1955 Laurence Wylie, Harvard's esteemed professor of French civilization, sent the manuscript of a sensitive chronicle of French country life, *A Village in the Vaucluse,* to Knopf. Back it came with a letter of rejection which said, "It is so far from being a book for the general reader that nothing can be done about it." Wylie did nothing "about" it—he sent it on to the Harvard University Press, which published it the next year. It became and has remained an extremely popular book for the general reader and the scholar alike.

ATLAS SHRUGGED
AYN RAND
1957

... the book is *much* too long. There are too many long speeches ... I regret to say that the book is unsaleable and unpublishable.

THE FOUNTAINHEAD
AYN RAND
1943

It is badly written and the hero is unsympathetic.

❧

This is a work of almost-genius—"genius" in the power of its expression—"almost" in the sense of its enormous bitterness. I wish there were an audience for a book of this kind. But there isn't. It won't sell.

❧

It is too intellectual for a novel.

CAPTAIN JANUARY
LAURA E. RICHARDS
1889

This is a small juvenile, written in an artificial and strained, not to say affected manner; and is neither fish, flesh nor fowl, not being suitable for children nor attractive to elders.

There is a half-baked belief among non-kitchen-minded folk that the culinary bible *Mastering the Art of French Cooking* was a much-wanted child, called into existence to satisfy a demand created by the popular TV series, *The French Chef.* Not so. *Mastering* started life as a twice-rejected orphan.

In 1953 a publisher signed a contract with Julia Child, Simone Beck, and Louisette Bertholle for a book with the working title *French Cooking for the American Kitchen.* Five years later the three cook-writers submitted their manuscript, an 850-page compendium called *French Sauces and French Poultry.* The publisher rejected it. The next year they brought back a drastically revised 684-page version titled *French Recipes for American Cooks.* The publisher rejected that too.

CASE IS CLOSED
MARY ROBERTS RINEHART
1957

I have read it, not once but twice, in an effort to find what you see in it, but I must be myopic.

ARUNDEL
KENNETH ROBERTS
1930

. . . not worth writing.

Knopf accepted it and published it in 1961 with the *Mastering* title. Though large and expensive, it sold fairly well right from the start. Impressed by the book's success, public television dreamed up the series *The French Chef,* starring Julia Child, which made its debut on February 11, 1963. That series was a smash hit from the cavalier flipping of that first-famous potato pancake onto the stove; *Mastering* mastered the air. That same year it was a Book-of-the-Month Club selection, and on November 25, 1966, Julia Child made the cover of *Time* magazine.

If the book (augmented by a second volume in 1970) were a record it would have gone platinum by now—it has sold more than a million copies.

THE TORRENT AND THE RIVER
EDWIN ARLINGTON ROBINSON
1896

We can only take refuge in the commonplace that it is next to impossible to publish successfully volumes of poems ... and we generally confine ourselves to the publication of books in whose success we can feel confidence.

VAN ZORN
EDWIN ARLINGTON ROBINSON
1914

I fancy the author of this tale reads Henry James diligently, and follows him at a *very* great distance . . . Everything is inferential, allusive, and comes to the point cautiously. The epigrams are of 'prentice-make, the humor crude, the wit invisible.

GOBLIN MARKET
CHRISTINA ROSSETTI
1862

She should exercise herself in the severest commonplace of meter until she can write as the public likes; then if she puts in her observation and passion all will become precious. But she must have Form first.

CALL IT SLEEP
HENRY ROTH
1935

As a practical commercial venture I am against it.

Memo from Joseph Hansen...

Now and then, the media have toyed with the notion of filming my books. My encounters with media people have all been preposterous and futile, but the memory I most treasure is of a meeting in a producer's office, where he suggested the way to begin the film was to have some clod in a bar call Dave Brandstetter a "faggot," and have Dave promptly knock him down with a hard right to the jaw. The producer's secretary glanced at me, and rolled her eyes at the ceiling. In the picture business intelligence and taste are to be found only among the office help. Count on it... It seems important to me that beginning writers ponder this—that since 1964, I have never had a book, story, or poem rejected that was not later published. If you know what you are doing, eventually you will run into an editor who knows what he/she is doing. It may take years, but never give up. Writing is a lonely business not just because you have to sit alone in a room with your machinery for hours and hours every day, month after month, year after year, but because after all the blood, sweat, toil, and tears you still have to find somebody who respects what you have written enough to leave it alone and print it. And, believe me, this remains true, whether the book is your first novel or your thirty-first.

The poet A. Wilber Stevens, later Dean of the College of Arts and Letters at the University of Nevada at Las Vegas, once sent a manuscript to the editor of a literary magazine whom he knew slightly. When his self-addressed return envelope came back to him he opened it and out fell a little pile of ashes.

CORNHUSKERS
CARL SANDBURG
1918

Good stuff, but rather out of our line. I dare you to do us a soft and luscious lyric, capable of reducing a fat woman to snuffles.

POEMS
GEORGE SANTAYANA
1922

We do not think we could sell a book of his poetry, in fact, we even fear its publication might retard his popularity.

SPECK, THE SPECIAL SARDINE
WILLIAM SAROYAN
1954

Even if Isaiah, William James, Confucius, Willa Cather and Mickey Spillane were to collaborate on an eleven-page story about a little sardine who didn't like being a sardine, and his little boy who didn't like being a little boy, I don't believe it would be a publishable book.

AND TO THINK THAT I SAW IT ON MULBERRY STREET
DR. SEUSS
1937

... too different from other juveniles on the market to warrant its selling.

THE IRRATIONAL KNOT
GEORGE BERNARD SHAW
1905

A novel of the most disagreeable kind ... the thought of the book is all wrong; the whole idea of it is odd, perverse and crude. It is the work of a man writing about life, when he knows nothing of it.

MAN AND SUPERMAN
GEORGE BERNARD SHAW
1905

... he will never be popular in the usual sense of the word, and perhaps scarcely remunerative.

AN UNSOCIAL SOCIALIST
GEORGE BERNARD SHAW
1885

. . . a whimsical and extravagant story, served up with a pungent literary sauce. The result is a dish, which I fancy only the few would relish.

GANDHI
WILLIAM SHIRER
1979

Too elementary.

In 1847 Charlotte Brontë (using the name Currer Bell) sent the manuscript of *The Professor* to a publishing house named Smith, Elder. That firm's letter of rejection actually encouraged the author: it discussed the book's merits and demerits "so courteously, so considerately, in a spirit so rational, with a discrimination so enlightened, that this very refusal cheered the author better than a vulgarly expressed acceptance would have done." (Later that same year Smith, Elder published *Jane Eyre*.)

Memo from Cyril Connolly:

As repressed sadists are supposed to become policemen or butchers, so those with irrational fear of life become publishers.

THE JUNGLE
UPTON SINCLAIR
1906

Sensational is a mild term for the book and the improbabilities are so glaring that even a boy reader would balk at them. It is fit only for the wastebasket.

❧

I advise without hesitation and unreservedly against the publication of this book ... it is gloom and horror unrelieved ... One feels that what is at the bottom of his fierceness is not nearly so much desire to help the poor as hatred of the rich ... As to the possibilities of a large sale, I should think them not very good.

IN MY FATHER'S COURT
ISAAC BASHEVIS SINGER
1966

Too pedestrian.

THE NEW MEN
C. P. SNOW
1954

It's polite, literate, plodding, sententious narrative of considerable competence but not a trace of talent or individuality; ... Real dull stuff for us Americans. The values in it are so bloody sanctimonious English that I found it hard to take.

THE MAKING OF AMERICANS
GERTRUDE STEIN
1925

We live in different worlds. Yours may hold the good, the beautiful, and the true, but if it does their guise is not for us to recognize. Those vedettes who lead the vanguard of picture arts are understood, or partly understood, over here by a reasonably compact following, but that following cannot translate their loyalties into a corresponding literature, and it would really be hopeless for us to set up this new standard.

THREE LIVES
GERTRUDE STEIN
1909

While it was conceded that there was present a literary reality—despite the foreignisms of the style—the readers felt that the strain of intensity was too unbroken and the portraits were over-complete and too infinitesimally detailed. A miniature may be overdone and apparently that is the way our readers felt about (this).

IDA: A NOVEL
GERTRUDE STEIN
1941

I am only one, only one, only. Only one being, one at the same time. Not two, not three, only one. Only one life to live, only sixty minutes in one hour. Only one pair of eyes. Only one brain. Only one being. Being only one, having only one pair of eyes, having only one time, having only one life, I cannot read your MS three or four times. Not even one time. Only one look, only one look is enough. Hardly one copy would sell here. Hardly one. Hardly one.

TRISTRAM SHANDY
LAURENCE STERNE
1759

To sport too much with your wit, or the game that wit has pointed out, is surfeiting; like toying with a man's mistress, it may be very delightful solacement to the inamorata, but little to the bystander.

A man supposedly sent a story to the *Reader's Digest* titled, "How I Made Love to a Bear." It was rejected. He rewrote it a little and retitled it "How I Made Love to a Bear in an Iron Lung" and sent it back. Again *Reader's Digest* rejected it. Another rewrite, another title change, to "How I Made Love to a Bear in an Iron Lung for the FBI," and another rejection. This time he didn't bother to rewrite at all—he just lengthened the title to "How I Made Love to a Bear in an Iron Lung for the FBI and Found God." Back came a telegram of acceptance.

LUST FOR LIFE
IRVING STONE
1934

A long, dull novel about an artist.

VALLEY OF THE DOLLS
JACQUELINE SUSANN
1966

... she is a painfully dull, inept, clumsy, undisciplined, rambling and thoroughly amateurish writer whose every sentence, paragraph and scene cries for the hand of a pro. She wastes endless pages on utter trivia, writes wide-eyed romantic scenes that would not make the back pages of *True Confessions,* hauls out every terrible show biz cliche in all the books, lets every good scene fall apart in endless talk and allows her book to ramble aimlessly... most of the first 200 pages are virtually worthless and dreadfully dull and practically every scene is dragged out flat and stomped on by her endless talk...

COLLECTED WORKS
J. M. SYNGE
1962

Undoubtedly they all have marked literary merit of a certain sort, but it is quite sure, it seems to me, that they would not in the slightest way appeal to the ordinary reading public of this country. For their sale you must depend on the little group of persons who are specially interested in the Irish Literary Movement or in odds and ends of pleasing literature.

"NOTUS IGNOTO"
BAYARD TAYLOR
1869

If the poem I have returned is really better than "The Sunshine of the Gods" I will eat a complete set of your works, and have dear old George Putnam thrown in for sauce. However, some day I hope to be out of this business, and quietly laid away in some uneditorial corner.

A CONFEDERACY OF DUNCES
JOHN KENNEDY TOOLE
1980

Obsessively foul and grotesque.

BARCHESTER TOWERS
ANTHONY TROLLOPE
1857

The grand defect of the work, I think, as a work of art is the low-mindedness and vulgarity of the chief actors. There is hardly a "lady" or "gentleman" among them.

"BROWN, JONES AND ROBINSON"
ANTHONY TROLLOPE
1863

You hit right and left—a wipe here, a sneer there, thrust a nasty *prong* into another place, cast a glow over Doctor Societies, a glory over balls till 4 in the morning,—in short, it is the old story—the shadow over the Church is broad and deep, and over every other quarter sunshine reigns—that is the *general impression* which the story gives, so far as it goes. There is nothing, of course, bad or vicious in it—that *could* not be, from you—but quite enough (and that without any necessity from your hand or heart) to keep [this magazine] and its Editor in boiling water until either were boiled to death.

Memo from Peter Dickinson ...

I've been fortunate enough to have received very few rejections, and think it likely that some of my acceptances may have been a bit pig-headed. Anything by way of crass rejection would have come from my own pen or typewriter, in the days when I used to read MSS for *Punch*. I probably sent out some couple of hundred rejections a week in those days. I remember one unfortunate contributor returned to me letters I had sent him several years apart, in both of which I used the same phrase about his contribution "not quite reaching flying-speed." Hell, there's a limit to what one can say about why a piece doesn't make one laugh. We had old-fashioned roll-top desks; mine jammed once, and in the process of mending it I found a rejection-slip penned by the great editor in the early part of this century, Owen Seaman, in which he said that he thought the article most amusing but could not publish it because he did not wish to encourage drunkenness among our troops in the trenches. No date, but it must have been during the 1914–18 war.

MANKIND IN THE MAKING
H. G. WELLS
1903

. . . only a minor writer of no large promise.

THE TIME MACHINE
H. G. WELLS
1895

It is not interesting enough for the general reader and not thorough enough for the scientific reader.

THE WAR OF THE WORLDS
H. G. WELLS
1898

An endless nightmare. I do not believe it would take . . . I think the verdict would be "Oh don't read that horrid book."

THE BOOK OF MERLYN
T. H. WHITE
1950

I do wish we could get you writing again on your nature subjects.

S mall, cosmetic changes can open doors. Long-mans, Green rejected a manuscript titled *The Problems of the Single Woman* only to see it become a bestseller after publication by another house as *Live Alone and Like It*. The same thing happened to a reject called *The Birds and the Bees*. It went on to prosper as *Everything You Always Wanted to Know About Sex but Were Afraid to Ask*.

LEAVES OF GRASS
WALT WHITMAN
1855

We deem it injudicious to commit ourselves.

LADY WINDERMERE'S FAN
OSCAR WILDE
1892

My dear sir,
I have read your manuscript. Oh, my dear sir.

THE PICTURE OF DORIAN GRAY
OSCAR WILDE
1891

It contains unpleasant elements.

THE DRAGON OF WONTLEY
OWEN WISTER
1892

A burlesque and grotesque piece of nonsense... it is mere fooling and does not have the bite and lasting quality of satire.

Memo from Simon Brett...

The only (rejection) I recall which rose above the boring was from a publisher to whom, in the late sixties or early seventies, I submitted yet another very properly unpublished novel. His reply ran: "I'm afraid the current state of the fiction market is too depressing for me to offer you any hope for this." I thought that was a very skillful rejection. While making it abundantly clear that my book had no chance at all, this situation was gracefully blamed by implication on outside factors rather than my own incompetence.

LOOK HOMEWARD, ANGEL
THOMAS WOLFE
1929

It is fearfully diffuse... In parts, it holds one's interest by its vitality, but it is marred by stylistic clichés, outlandish adjectives and similes, etc. I do not believe it would be possible or worthwhile to doctor this up. It has all the faults of youth and inexperience.

❧

... we just can't see it. It is so long—so terribly long—that it is most difficult for a reader to sustain an interest to the end. One cannot deny that much of it has quality, if not originality—the autobiography of a young man—and so much of it has been done, and so often, that we hesitate to take another chance. We had four books of this type last year, and each one failed... it isn't a matter of carefully editing it, or publishing it in an abridged form, it is the whole thing that must be considered. I am sorry about all this, but, having this attitude, nothing is left for us to do but decline it...

❧

Terrible.

❧

What the manuscript lacked basically was a shape... what was important lost its full effect because of intrusions of the commonplace.

So many books rejected by so many publishers so many times—how do those murdering bastards *feel* when they strangle yet another unborn child? William Styron's 1979 novel, *Sophie's Choice,* tells it like it was in 1947 when the hero was a forty-dollar-a-week reader for McGraw-Hill. The "lusterless drudgery" of trudging through the "club-footed syntax" and "unrelenting mediocrity" of manuscripts like *Tall Grows the Eelgrass,* by Edmonia Biersticker ("fiction ... may be the worst novel ever penned by woman or beast. Decline with all possible speed"), and *The Plumber's Wench,* by Audrey Smillie ("... absolutely imperative that this book never be published"), so stupefied the poor wretch that when a manuscript about a "long, solemn, and tedious Pacific voyage" made by "men adrift on a raft" fell into his hands he recommended rejection—"maybe a university press would buy it, but it's definitely not for us"—and the book was *Kon-Tiki.*

POEMS
WILLIAM BUTLER YEATS
1895

I am relieved to find the critics shrink from saying that Mr. Yeats will ever be a popular author. I should really at last despair of mankind, if he could be . . . absolutely empty and void. The work does not please the ear, nor kindle the imagination, nor hint a thought for one's reflection . . . Do what I will, I can see no sense in the thing: it is to me sheer nonsense. I do not say it is obscure, or uncouth or barbaric or affected—tho' it is all these evil things; I say it is to me absolute nullity . . . I would not read a page of it again for worlds.

ᔍ

That he has any real paying audience I find hard to believe.

Publishers say, somewhat defensively, that their rejections are different from those of other rejecters, not necessarily based on value judgements. They may like a manuscript, they say, but be unable to publish it because of prior commitments or scheduling jams or lack of money or other such operational obstacles. Still and all, they have let some amazingly big fish slip through their nets, ultimate blockbusters of all varieties: *War and Peace, The Good Earth, The Sun Is My Undoing, The Fountainhead, To Kill a Mockingbird, Rubáiyát, Watership Down* . . . The list goes on and on.

PUSHCART'S
COMPLETE
ROTTEN REVIEWS
&
REJECTIONS
was designed by CMYK Design
Ossining, New York

PUSHCART PRESS